PEARSON EDEXCEL INTERNATIONAL GCSE (9–1)

HISTORY
A DIVIDED UNION: CIVIL RIGHTS IN THE USA, 1945–74
Student Book

Kirsty Taylor

Series Editor: Nigel Kelly

Published by Pearson Education Limited, 80 Strand, London, WC2R 0RL.

www.pearsonglobalschools.com

Copies of official specifications for all Pearson qualifications may be found on the website: https://qualifications.pearson.com

Text © Pearson Education Limited 2017
Edited by Paul Martin and Stephanie White
Designed by Cobalt id and Pearson Education Limited
Typeset and illustrated by Phoenix Photosetting Ltd, Chatham, Kent
Original illustrations © Pearson Education Limited 2017
Cover design by Pearson Education Limited
Picture research by Andreas Schindler
Cover photo/illustration Mary Evans Picture Library: INTERFOTO AGENTUR
Inside front cover: **Shutterstock.com:** Dmitry Lobanov

The rights of Kirsty Taylor to be identified as author of this work have been asserted by her in accordance with the Copyright, Designs and Patents Act 1988.

First published 2017

24
10

British Library Cataloguing in Publication Data
A catalogue record for this book is available from the British Library

ISBN 978 0 435 18536 7

Printed in Great Britain by Bell and Bain Ltd, Glasgow

Acknowledgements
The author and publisher would like to thank the following for permission to reproduce their photographs:
(Key: b-bottom; c-centre; l-left; r-right; t-top)

Alamy Stock Photo: Everett Collection Historical 11c, 35tr, 36bl, 100 (b), 100 (j), Everett Collection Inc 10br, 33tr, ivbr, Glasshouse Images 100 (h), Granger Historical Picture Archive 24br, 48tr, 64tr, 105tr, Heritage Image Partnership Ltd 84br, LOC Photo 52t, RBM Vintage Images 100 (i), World History Archive 62cr, ZUMA Press, Inc. 100 (k); **Getty Images:** AFP 42, Afro American Newspapers / Gado 28tr, Bettmann 72, 78bl, 98br, 100 (a), 100 (c), 100 (d), Tim Chapman 100 (e), Eugene Gordon / The New York Historical Society 88tr, Peter Keegan / Keystone 89bc, Keystone 100 (l), Wally McNamee / Corbis 101br, Gjon Mili / The LIFE Picture Collection 100 (f), Charles Moore 20, New York Post Archives 76bl, Bill Pierce / The LIFE Images Collection 96, 103br, Howard Ruffner 81t, Ted Streshinsky / Corbis 77br, ullstein bild 26b, Underwood Archives 2, 60bl, Universal History Archive 55t, Universal History Archive / UIG 5bl, Grey Villet / The LIFE Picture Collection 30cl, Hank Walker / The LIFE Picture Collection 15tr, 23bl, 23br; **Magnum Photos Ltd:** Elliott Erwitt 21br; **Mary Evans Picture Library:** Everett Collection 51tr **Science Source:** Bruce Roberts / Photo Researchers, Inc. 44tr; **Paul Szep:** 91cr; **Telegraph Media Group:** / British Cartoon Archive, University of Kent www.cartoons.ac.uk 81br; **The Herb Block Foundation:** A 1961 Herblock Cartoon, © The Herb Block Foundation 46bc; **TopFoto:** Mark Godfrey / The Image Works 99cl, Lisa Law / The Image Works 83tr, UPP 100 (g)

All other images © Pearson Education

We are grateful to the following for permission to reproduce copyright material:

Text
Extract on page 7, courtesy of the Harry S. Truman Library and Museum; Extract on page 7 from United States 1917–2008 and Civil Rights 1865–1992. Reprinted by permission of HarperCollins Publishers Ltd, copyright 2008 D. Murphy & K. Cooper; Extract on page 15 CBS News; Extract on page 16 from United States 1917–2008 and Civil Rights 1865–1992. Reprinted by permission of HarperCollins Publishers Ltd, copyright 2008 D. Murphy & K. Cooper; Extract on page 27 The publisher wishes to thank The National Association for the Advancement of Colored People, for authorizing the use of this statement.; Extract on page 29 Reprinted by permission of The University of Tennessee Press. From Jo Ann Gibson Robinson's The Montgomery Bus Boycott and the Women Who Started It: The Memoir of Jo Ann Gibson Robinson, edited, with a foreword, by David G. Garrow. Copyright © 1987 by The University of Tennessee Press.; Extract on page 32 from Edexcel GCSE History : CA6 Government and protest in the USA 1945–70 Controlled Assessment Student by A Leonard, C Warren, R Bircher, D Magnoff, J Shuter, 2010, Pearson Education Limited; Extracts on page 37 from Edexcel GCSE History : CA6 Government and protest in the USA 1945–70 Controlled Assessment Student by A Leonard, C Warren, R Bircher, D Magnoff, J Shuter, 2010, Pearson Education Limited; Extract on page 38 from The Penguin History of the United States of America, H. Brogan, 1985, Pearson Education Limited.; Extract on page 45 from WE AIN'T WHAT WE OUGHT TO BE: THE BLACK FREEDOM STRUGGLE FROM EMANCIPATION TO OBAMA by Stephen Tuck, Cambridge, Mass.: The Belknap Press of Harvard University Press, Copyright © 2010 by Stephen Tuck.; Extract on page 47 from United States 1917–2008 and Civil Rights 1865–1992. Reprinted by permission of HarperCollins Publishers Ltd, copyright 2008 D. Murphy & K. Cooper.; Extract on page 49 from United States 1917–2008 and Civil Rights 1865–1992. Reprinted by permission of HarperCollins Publishers Ltd, copyright 2008 D. Murphy & K. Cooper.; Extract on page 53 Reprinted by arrangement with The Heirs to the Estate of Martin Luther King Jr., c/o Writers House as agent for the proprietor New York, NY.; Copyright 1963 Dr. Martin Luther King Jr. Copyright renewed 1991 Conetta Scott King; Extract on page 60 from By Any Means Necessary: Speeches, Interviews, and a Letter by Malcolm X, Copyright © 1970, 1992 by Betty Shabazz and Pathfinder Press Reprinted by permission.; Extract on page 65 from E. Wright, 1996, The American Dream, John Wiley and Sons; Extract on page 76 from Edexcel GCSE Modern World History Unit 3C A Divided Union? The USA 1945–70. J. Shuter, 2009, Pearson Education Limited.; Extract on page 77 from a speech by Mario Savio, used with permission by Lynne Hollander Savio; Extract on page 80 from The Right of Protest and Civil Disobedience, Indiana Law Journal, Vol. 41, Issue 2, H.A Freeman 1966, by permission of Indiana University Trustees; Extract on page 83 from an online portfolio of the creative works of Emily Marsden, used by kind permission of Emily Marsden; Extract on page 86 from THE FEMININE MYSTIQUE by Betty Friedan. Copyright © 1983, 1974, 1973, 1963 by Betty Friedan. Used by permission of W. W. Norton & Company, Inc. and Orion Publishing Group, London Copyright 1963 Reprinted by permission of Curtis Brown, Ltd.; Extract on page 89 from The Bra Burners by Art Buchwald, permission kindly granted by Joel Buchwald; Extract on page 90 from OCR History A Civil Rights in the USA 1865–1991, D. Paterson et al, Pearson Education Limited; Extract on page 97 from Memories of Richard Nixon, Maurice Stans, Nixon Presidency: twenty-two intimate perspectives of Richard M. Nixon, University Press of America, used by permission Rowman & Littlefield Publishing Group, University Press of America; Extract on page 98 from the New York Times, 30 June, copyright 2007 The New York Times. All rights reserved. Used by permission and protected by the Copyright Laws of the United States. The printing, copying, redistribution, or retransmission of this Content without express written permission is prohibited.; Extract on page 100 from Letter from James W. McCord, Jr., to Judge John Sirica, March 19, 1973, filed in: United States v. George Gordon Liddy, et al., C.R. 1827–72, United States District Court for the District of Columbia; Records of District Courts of the United States, Record Group 21; NARA, College Park, MD.; Extract on page 101 from the Washington Post, 3 June, copyright 1973 The Washington Post. All rights reserved. Used by permission and protected by the Copyright Laws of the United States. The printing, copying, redistribution, or retransmission of this Content without express written permission in prohibited.; Extract on page 105 from The Telegraph, J. Aitken. Telegraph Media Group Ltd 2013; Extract on page 106 from GCSE Modern World History 2nd Edition, Ben Walsh. Reproduced by permission of Hodder Education.

Select glossary terms have been taken from The Longman Dictionary of Contemporary English Online.

Disclaimer
All maps in this book are drawn to support the key learning points. They are illustrative in style and are not exact representations.

Endorsement statement
In order to ensure that this resource offers high-quality support for the associated Pearson qualification, it has been through a review process by the awarding body. This process confirms that this resource fully covers the teaching and learning content of the specification or part of a specification at which it is aimed. It also confirms that it demonstrates an appropriate balance between the development of subject skills, knowledge and understanding, in addition to preparation for assessment.

Endorsement does not cover any guidance on assessment activities or processes (e.g. practice questions or advice on how to answer assessment questions), included in the resource nor does it prescribe any particular approach to the teaching or delivery of a related course.

While the publishers have made every attempt to ensure that advice on the qualification and its assessment is accurate, the official specification and associated assessment guidance materials are the only authoritative source of information and should always be referred to for definitive guidance.

Pearson examiners have not contributed to any sections in this resource relevant to examination papers for which they have responsibility.

Examiners will not use endorsed resources as a source of material for any assessment set by Pearson. Endorsement of a resource does not mean that the resource is required to achieve this Pearson qualification, nor does it mean that it is the only suitable material available to support the qualification, and any resource lists produced by the awarding body shall include this and other appropriate resources.

CONTENTS

ABOUT THIS BOOK

This book is written for students following the Pearson Edexcel International GCSE (9–1) History specification and covers one unit of the course. This unit is A Divided Union: Civil Rights in the USA, 1945–74, one of the Depth Studies.

The History course has been structured so that teaching and learning can take place in any order, both in the classroom and in any independent learning. The book contains five chapters which match the five areas of content in the specification:

- The Red Scare and McCarthyism
- Civil rights in the 1950s
- The impact of civil rights protests, 1960–74
- Other protest movements: students, women, anti–Vietnam
- Nixon and Watergate

Each chapter is split into multiple sections to break down content into manageable chunks and to ensure full coverage of the specification.

Each chapter features a mix of learning and activities. Sources are embedded throughout to develop your understanding and exam-style questions help you to put learning into practice. Recap pages at the end of each chapter summarise key information and let you check your understanding. Exam guidance pages help you prepare confidently for the exam.

Learning Objectives Each section starts with a list of what you will learn in it. They are carefully tailored to address key assessment objectives central to the course.

Activity Each chapter includes activities to help check and embed knowledge and understanding.

Source Photos, cartoons and text sources are used to explain events and show you what people from the period said, thought or created, helping you to build your understanding.

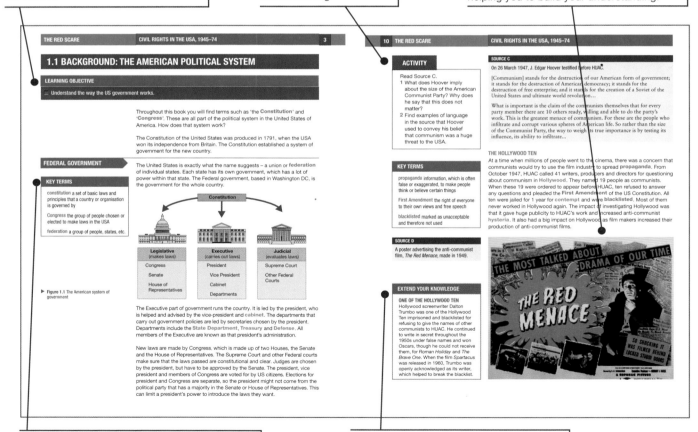

Key term Useful words and phrases are colour coded within the main text and picked out in the margin with concise and simple definitions. These help understanding of key subject terms and support students whose first language is not English.

Extend your knowledge Interesting facts to encourage wider thought and stimulate discussion. They are closely related to key issues and allow you to add depth to your knowledge and answers.

Hint
All exam-style questions are accompanied by a hint to help you get started on an answer.

Recap
At the end of each chapter, you will find a page designed to help you consolidate and reflect on the chapter as a whole.

Recall quiz
This quick quiz is ideal for checking your knowledge or for revision.

Exam-style question
Questions tailored to the Pearson Edexcel specification to allow for practice and development of exam writing technique. They also allow for practice responding to the command words used in the exams.

Skills
Relevant exam questions have been assigned the key skills which you will gain from undertaking them, allowing for a strong focus on particular academic qualities. These transferable skills are highly valued in further study and the workplace.

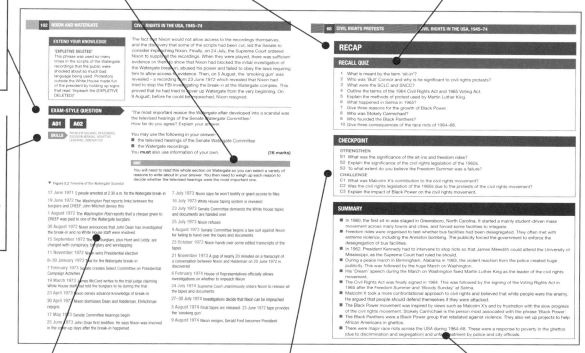

Timeline
Visual representation of events to clarify the order in which they happened.

Checkpoint
Checkpoints help you to check and reflect on your learning. The Strengthen section helps you to consolidate knowledge and understanding, and check that you have grasped the basic ideas and skills. The Challenge questions push you to go beyond just understanding the information, and into evaluation and analysis of what you have studied.

Summary
The main points of each chapter are summarised in a series of bullet points. These are great for embedding core knowledge and handy for revision.

Exam guidance
At the end of each chapter, you will find two pages designed to help you better understand the exam questions and how to answer them. Each exam guidance section focuses on a particular question type that you will find in the exam, allowing you to approach them with confidence.

Student answers
Exemplar student answers are used to show what an answer to the exam question may look like. There are often two levels of answers so you can see what you need to do to write better responses.

Advice on answering the question
Three key questions about the exam question are answered here in order to explain what the question is testing and what you need to do to succeed in the exam.

Pearson Progression
Sample student answers have been given a Pearson step from 1 to 12. This tells you how well the response has met the criteria in the Pearson Progression Map.

Commentary
Feedback on the quality of the answer is provided to help you understand their strengths and weaknesses and show how they can be improved.

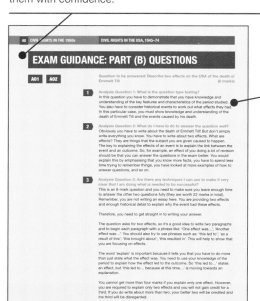

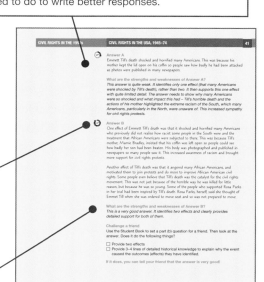

TIMELINE – A DIVIDED UNION: CIVIL RIGHTS IN THE USA, 1945–74

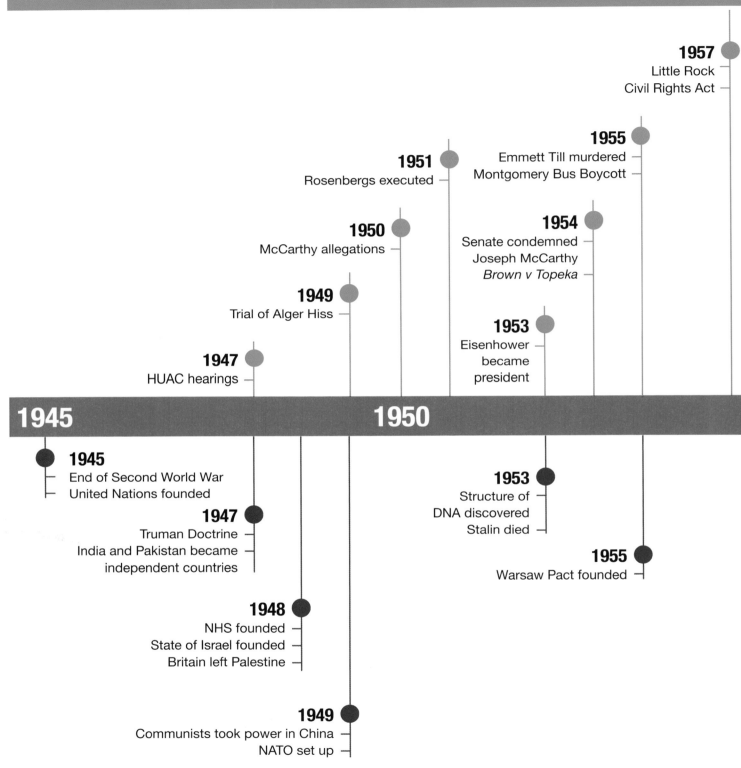

1957
Little Rock
Civil Rights Act

1955
Emmett Till murdered
Montgomery Bus Boycott

1951
Rosenbergs executed

1954
Senate condemned
Joseph McCarthy
Brown v Topeka

1950
McCarthy allegations

1949
Trial of Alger Hiss

1953
Eisenhower
became
president

1947
HUAC hearings

1945   1950

1945
End of Second World War
United Nations founded

1947
Truman Doctrine
India and Pakistan became
independent countries

1953
Structure of
DNA discovered
Stalin died

1948
NHS founded
State of Israel founded
Britain left Palestine

1955
Warsaw Pact founded

1949
Communists took power in China
NATO set up

TIMELINE – WORLD

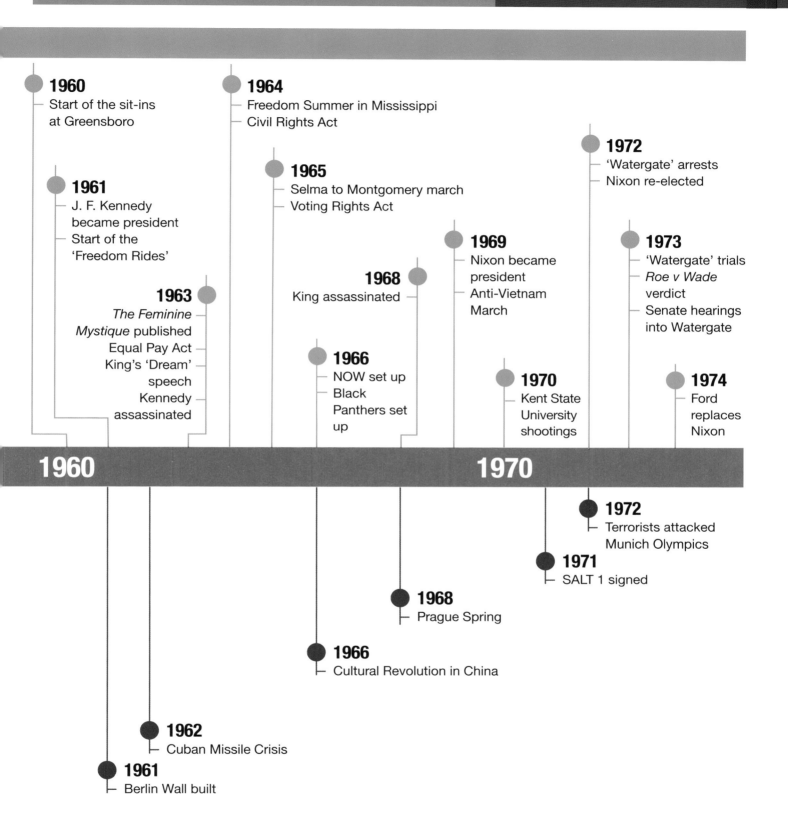

1960
Start of the sit-ins
at Greensboro

1961
J. F. Kennedy
became president
Start of the
'Freedom Rides'

1963
*The Feminine
Mystique* published
Equal Pay Act
King's 'Dream'
speech
Kennedy
assassinated

1964
Freedom Summer in Mississippi
Civil Rights Act

1965
Selma to Montgomery march
Voting Rights Act

1968
King assassinated

1966
NOW set up
Black
Panthers set
up

1969
Nixon became
president
Anti-Vietnam
March

1970
Kent State
University
shootings

1972
'Watergate' arrests
Nixon re-elected

1973
'Watergate' trials
Roe v Wade
verdict
Senate hearings
into Watergate

1974
Ford
replaces
Nixon

1960

1970

1972
Terrorists attacked
Munich Olympics

1971
SALT 1 signed

1968
Prague Spring

1966
Cultural Revolution in China

1962
Cuban Missile Crisis

1961
Berlin Wall built

1. THE RED SCARE AND MCCARTHYISM

LEARNING OBJECTIVES

☐ Understand the reasons for the Red Scare, including the Cold War

☐ Understand the impact of events in the USA on the Red Scare

☐ Understand the role of McCarthy and the impact of McCarthyism on the USA.

Following the 1917 Russian revolution, many Americans feared the spread of communism. After 1945, this fear increased dramatically due to the spreading influence of the Soviet Union and the events of the Cold War. Many people believed that a communist takeover of the USA was a real possibility. Thousands of people were questioned in private and public hearings and, sometimes with false evidence, some went to criminal trials and were convicted. Cases such as the Hollywood Ten, Alger Hiss and the Rosenbergs seemed to prove to many that the communist threat was very real. Thousands of people lost their jobs, some with very little proof they had done anything wrong.

Encouraged by individuals and agencies such as the FBI, fear and suspicion of people who could be communist spies gripped the nation. As communists were known as 'reds', this became known as the Red Scare. The Red Scare reached a peak of total hysteria in the early 1950s, largely due to the actions of Senator Joseph McCarthy.

1.1 BACKGROUND: THE AMERICAN POLITICAL SYSTEM

LEARNING OBJECTIVE

☐ Understand the way the US government works.

Throughout this book you will find terms such as 'the **Constitution**' and '**Congress**'. These are all part of the political system in the United States of America. How does that system work?

The Constitution of the United States was produced in 1791, when the USA won its independence from Britain. The Constitution established a system of government for the new country.

FEDERAL GOVERNMENT

The United States is exactly what the name suggests – a union or **federation** of individual states. Each state has its own government, which has a lot of power within that state. The Federal government, based in Washington DC, is the government for the whole country.

KEY TERMS

constitution a set of basic laws and principles that a country or organisation is governed by

Congress the group of people chosen or elected to make laws in the USA

federation a group of people, states, etc.

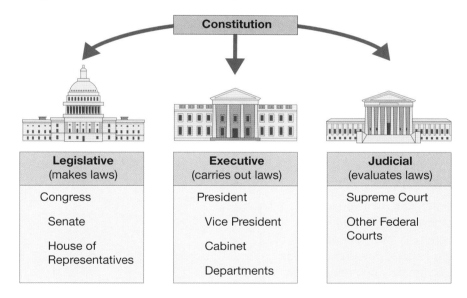

▶ **Figure 1.1** The American system of government

The Executive part of government runs the country. It is led by the president, who is helped and advised by the vice-president and **cabinet**. The departments that carry out government policies are led by secretaries chosen by the president. Departments include the **State Department**, **Treasury** and **Defense**. All members of the Executive are known as that president's administration.

New laws are made by Congress, which is made up of two Houses, the Senate and the House of Representatives. The Supreme Court and other Federal courts make sure that the laws passed are constitutional and clear. Judges are chosen by the president, but have to be approved by the Senate. The president, vice president and members of Congress are voted for by US citizens. Elections for president and Congress are separate, so the president might not come from the political party that has a majority in the Senate or House of Representatives. This can limit a president's power to introduce the laws they want.

The US system of government was designed to limit the powers of each group or person, including the president. For example, laws passed by Congress can be **vetoed** by either the president or the Supreme Court but Congress can **impeach** the president and Supreme Court judges and remove them from office.

STATE GOVERNMENTS

KEY TERMS

impeach prosecute a person in government for misconduct while in office

amendments (political) changes to a bill or constitution

ratified given formal approval

Each state government also has its own political system, with a governor, a **legislature** and a supreme court. While the Federal government is responsible for foreign policy and some **taxation**, state governments have control over most of the laws that apply within each state. Examples include laws on education and use of the **death penalty**. In the period of this book, 'states' rights' was a cry often heard by those trying to prevent a Federal law being passed or to defend a state law. Each state also has a National Guard, commanded by the governor, to enforce the law. This armed force can be taken over by the president in an emergency.

AMENDMENTS TO THE CONSTITUTION

There have only been 27 additions or **amendments** to the US Constitution. An amendment to the Constitution requires a two-thirds majority of both Houses of Congress and has to be **ratified** by three-quarters of the states. The first ten amendments were ratified months after the Constitution was made final and set out the rights of all US citizens. The other amendments have made changes to the system of government or added new rights for citizens. Amendments will be mentioned frequently in this book.

▶ **Figure 1.2** Examples of amendments to the US Constitution

ACTIVITY

1 Draw your own version of Figure 1.1, including a summary of what each part of the Federal government does.
2 Explain why someone might be committing a crime in one state of the USA but not in another state.

Amendment 1 (1791):
Freedom of religion, speech and the press, and the right to gather peacefully and petition the government

Amendment 2 (1791):
The right of the people to keep and bear arms

Amendment 6 (1791):
The right to a fair trial with an impartial jury

Amendment 13 (1865):
Abolition of slavery

Amendment 14 (1868):
Civil rights for all American citizens – equal protection of the law

Amendment 15 (1870):
Granting African American men the right to vote

Amendment 19 (1920):
Granting women the right to vote

Amendment 24 (1964):
Banned the use of a poll tax (or other tax) for voter registration

1.2 REASONS FOR THE RED SCARE: THE COLD WAR

LEARNING OBJECTIVES

- Understand how the Cold War developed
- Understand how the Cold War led to the Red Scare in the USA
- Understand how the events of the Cold War increased the fear of communism in the USA.

In 1945, the Second World War came to an end when the USA and its **allies** (including Britain and the **Soviet Union**) defeated Germany and Japan. The USA and the Soviet Union had emerged as the two most powerful nations in the world. They may have fought on the same side since 1941, but there was much distrust between the two **superpowers**. In the years following the end of the Second World War, this distrust developed into the **Cold War**.

COMMUNISM VERSUS CAPITALISM

KEY TERMS

capitalist someone who supports capitalism, an economic and political system in which businesses belong mostly to private owners, not to the government

communist someone who supports communism, a political system in which the government controls the production of food and goods and there is no privately owned property

The USA is a **capitalist** democracy. This means that the government is voted for by people during regular elections and that businesses are owned privately by individuals, largely free of government control. In a **communist** state, the only candidates in elections are communist and businesses are owned and run by the government.

In the revolution of 1917, the Russian **Empire** was taken over by communists. Shortly after this, there was a wave of anti-communist violence across the USA, which led to the first Red Scare of 1919–20. Many Americans feared immigrants from Eastern Europe would try to take over their government and make the USA communist as well. Thousands of suspected communists were arrested and some Russian immigrants were sent back to Russia. Although fear of communism in the USA did reduce after 1920, it did not disappear completely and many Americans remained concerned that the Soviet Union wanted to destroy capitalism.

American fears of a communist takeover were not completely without basis. One of the stated aims of some Russian communists in 1917 had been world revolution and to encourage communism in other countries. In contrast, the USA wanted the rest of the world to be capitalist because it needed other countries to trade with so its businesses and people would grow richer.

SOURCE A

The front cover of a magazine sold and given away free by a church group in the USA in the 1940s and 1950s.

EXTEND YOUR KNOWLEDGE

THE 'RED' SCARE
The colour red was used instead of the word 'communist' in many instances such as the 'Red' Scare and 'Red' Menace. Red was the main colour in the flags of the communist Soviet Union and Chinese communists who were trying to win the Chinese civil war. The colour red has long been associated with left-wing groups, going back to the 18th century. Some historians believe the colour red was chosen to represent the blood of the workers who died in the 'war' against capitalism.

THE COLD WAR BEGINS

ACTIVITY

Start to create your own timeline of the Cold War and Red Scare. On an A3 piece of paper, draw a vertical line down the centre and mark the years 1945 to 1955, making sure there's plenty of room to write events for each year.

As you read through this section, complete the left-hand side of the timeline with the international events that added to the fear of communism in the USA.

In the last months of the Second World War, Eastern Europe had been liberated from the **Nazis** by the Red Army of the Soviet Union. When the war was over, Soviet **troops** remained in the liberated countries. Between February and July 1945, communist governments were set up in some of these countries (see Figure 1.3). To Soviets, this provided a **buffer zone** of protection against another invasion from the west – up to 25 million Soviets had been killed in the Second World War. However, to many in Western Europe and the USA, it looked like the Soviet Union was trying to take over Europe.

On 16 July 1945, the USA successfully tested an **atomic bomb**. Despite being allies, the Soviet Union had not been told that the USA was developing this technology and saw it as a threat. On 6 and 9 August, the US Air Force dropped two atomic bombs on Japan and the whole world witnessed the horror and devastation. Stalin, leader of the Soviet Union, immediately boosted the Soviet atomic research programme with money and scientists to try to develop his own bomb as soon as possible.

SOVIET EXPANSION IN EUROPE

In 1946, communists in Greece tried to take over the government. Although the Soviet Union did not send materials or troops to help the Greek communists, it did voice encouragement. This added to American fears of a communist takeover of Europe, so the US government sent money to the Greek government to remove the communists. Throughout 1947 and 1948,

▶ **Figure 1.3** Soviet expansion in Europe by 1950

- — 'Iron Curtain'
- ▦ Territories occupied by the Soviet Union in 1945
- ▤ Communist takeover
- ▨ 'Free' elections

EXTEND YOUR KNOWLEDGE

A GIFT FROM THE SOVIET UNION
In 1946, the US ambassador to the Soviet Union was given a wooden copy of the Great Seal of the USA as a gift from the Soviet Union. In 1952, a listening device was discovered hidden inside the Great Seal – the Soviets had been able to hear everything that had been said in the US ambassador's office for nearly 6 years!

the remaining countries under Soviet influence in Eastern Europe became communist. Some were taken over by force while others held elections in which the only candidates allowed to stand were members of the Communist Party. By 1950, all the countries of of Eastern Europe had communist governments and most had become **satellite states** of the Soviet Union.

THE TRUMAN DOCTRINE AND MARSHALL PLAN

SOURCE B

From the speech where President Truman announced the Truman Doctrine, 12 March 1947.

Today, nearly every nation must choose between opposing ways of life. I believe the US must support peoples resisting attempted control by armed minorities or outside pressures. I believe our help should be mainly economic aid to restore economic stability and orderly [well-organised] political progress.

To try to prevent more countries becoming communist, in March 1947, the US government, led by President Truman, announced the Truman Doctrine. This promised help to support any country resisting takeover by other groups or countries (by which they meant communists). In other words, the USA would help any country at risk of a communist takeover. The US government decided to back up the Truman Doctrine with financial help in the belief that communist ideas were more likely to take hold in areas of poverty. The Marshall Plan therefore gave millions of dollars of aid to many European countries suffering from economic problems after the Second World War. The Soviet Union saw this as the USA trying to extend its influence and Stalin did not allow Eastern European countries to accept the aid offered.

EXTRACT A

From a modern textbook.

Even though there was pressure on Truman at home, he did deliberately exaggerate the threat of communism to get support for his policy in Greece and to get the Truman Doctrine passed [through Congress]. He and Secretary of State, Dean Acheson, exploited the Soviet threat as they wanted the United States to take a more active and forceful role in the world. This included 'getting tough with Russia', as Truman put it in 1946. It was time he said to 'stop babying the Soviets' [treating them so well].

EXAM-STYLE QUESTION

AO4

SKILLS ▷ ANALYSIS, INTERPRETATION, CREATIVITY

Study Extract A.

What impression does the author give about the US government and the threat of communism?

You **must** use Extract A to explain your answer. **(6 marks)**

HINT

In questions asking 'what impression' does the author give, it is a good idea to choose language from the extract to illustrate your point.

THE BERLIN CRISIS

It was in Germany in 1948–49 that it looked as though the Cold War might turn into a 'Hot' War, with armed conflict. In 1945, Germany had been split into four, with the USA, the Soviet Union, France and the UK each controlling a zone. The German capital, Berlin, was also divided into four zones, but the city was inside the Soviet zone of Germany. In 1946, without consulting the Soviet Union, Britain, France and the USA combined their zones into one area that later became West Germany. By 1948, there were signs that the western zone of Germany was beginning to recover from the effects of the war. The Soviet Union feared the threat of a recovered Germany.

In June 1948, Stalin blocked all road, rail and canal supply lines into West Berlin in an attempt to make the whole of Berlin dependent on the Soviet Union and free from Western influence. President Truman saw this as a test of the Truman

Doctrine. He was not prepared to leave West Berlin to become communist and the Western allies decided to take supplies by aircraft into the city. Stalin knew that firing on the aeroplanes would start a war so there was nothing he could do. In May 1949, he reopened the supply lines. To the Soviets, this was a moral defeat and also left Berlin as a crisis point in the years to come.

THE COLD WAR ESCALATES

The events of 1949–50 convinced many Americans, including people in government, that the Soviet Union wanted world domination. It was providing support for the communists in the Chinese civil war and to North Korea in its attempt to take over South Korea. Despite substantial US support for their opponents, the Chinese communists won the civil war and took control of China in 1949. There were other communist uprisings in Malaya, Indonesia, Burma and the Philippines. Then, in 1950, communist North Korea invaded capitalist South Korea. The US government persuaded the United Nations to send military help to South Korea. The United Nations forces came from 15 different countries, but the vast majority were American. North Korea, on the other hand, was supported by the Soviet Union. The UN forces managed to push the North Korean forces back beyond the original border, threatening China. This provoked the Chinese into joining the war in support of North Korea and the UN forces were forced back to the original border. Neither side made further gains despite 2 more years of conflict. Fighting ended in July 1953.

Another very important development was the Soviet Union successfully testing its own atomic bomb in August 1949. Americans were shocked and afraid – their country's biggest enemy now had a weapon capable of huge destruction. The world suddenly appeared to be a far more dangerous place.

ACTIVITY

1 In pairs, discuss the impact of each of the international events below on people in the USA. How would each crisis have made US citizens feel?
 ■ Eastern Europe becoming communist
 ■ communist uprising in Greece
 ■ the Berlin Crisis
 ■ communist uprisings in Asia
 ■ China becoming communist
 ■ Soviets developing the atomic bomb
 ■ the Korean War.
2 Decide which of the events listed in question 1 caused the biggest fear of communism in the USA. Give reasons for your choice.

EXAM-STYLE QUESTION

A01 **A02**

Explain **two** effects of the Cold War on the USA.   **(8 marks)**

HINT

This question is about the impact of events. You need to give two effects, with supporting details for each one.

1.3 REASONS FOR THE RED SCARE: EVENTS IN THE USA

LEARNING OBJECTIVES

- Understand the increase of anti-communism in the USA due to the work of the FBI
- Understand the influence of HUAC, including the case of the Hollywood Ten, on the Red Scare
- Understand the impact of the Hiss and Rosenberg cases on the Red Scare.

ACTIVITY

As you read through this section, complete the right-hand side of the timeline you started on page 6, with the events of the Red Scare in the USA.

THE ROLE OF THE FBI

KEY TERMS

Federal Bureau of Investigation the USA's domestic intelligence and security service

hearings where evidence is presented and people testify to a court or government body; not the same as a criminal trial

intelligence (n, political) information about the secret activities of foreign governments, the military plans of an enemy, etc.

The director of the **Federal Bureau of Investigation** was J. Edgar Hoover. He had very strong anti-communist views and played a major role in arresting suspected communists during the first Red Scare of 1919–20 (see page 5). As the Cold War began, the FBI started creating files of evidence on those it suspected of spying for communist Russia.

FEDERAL LOYALTY BOARDS

Hoover was concerned about communist spies working within Federal government departments and wrote to President Truman stating his belief that this was a serious problem. In response, in March 1947, Truman gave an order that allowed government employees to be removed from their posts if there were 'reasonable grounds' to believe they were disloyal to the United States.

Hoover's FBI then set up Federal Loyalty Boards to investigate government employees to find out if they were communists or had links to communism. Between 1947 and 1951, around 3 million government workers were investigated and up to 3,000 people were either fired or forced to resign because they were considered to be a security risk. However, no evidence of actual spying was found.

As fear of communism grew, many states, cities and even private businesses investigated their workforce and thousands of employees, some of whom were only suspected of being sympathetic to communists, lost their jobs.

HOUSE COMMITTEE ON UN-AMERICAN ACTIVITIES

The House Committee on Un-American Activities (known as HUAC) had been set up by the US government in 1938 to monitor extremist groups suspected of 'Un-American' activities. Members of Congress were selected to be on the committee. In the climate of 1947, it began public hearings on the threat presented by the Communist Party of America. Hoover was the most important witness (see Source C) and saw HUAC's potential in educating the public and exposing traitors. The FBI began secretly passing intelligence to HUAC. HUAC then called suspected communists and witnesses to be questioned. The committee asked suspects, 'Are you now or have you ever been a member of the Communist Party?' and sent people for criminal trial depending on the answers they received.

ACTIVITY

Read Source C.

1 What does Hoover imply about the size of the American Communist Party? Why does he say that this does not matter?

2 Find examples of language in the source that Hoover used to convey his belief that communism was a huge threat to the USA.

KEY TERMS

propaganda information, which is often false or exaggerated, to make people think or believe certain things

First Amendment the right of everyone to their own views and free speech

blacklisted marked as unacceptable and therefore not used

SOURCE D

A poster advertising the anti-communist film, *The Red Menace*, made in 1949.

EXTEND YOUR KNOWLEDGE

ONE OF THE HOLLYWOOD TEN
Hollywood screenwriter Dalton Trumbo was one of the Hollywood Ten imprisoned and blacklisted for refusing to give the names of other communists to HUAC. He continued to write in secret throughout the 1950s under false names and won Oscars, though he could not receive them, for *Roman Holiday* and *The Brave One*. When the film *Spartacus* was released in 1960, Trumbo was openly acknowledged as its writer, which helped to break the blacklist.

SOURCE C

On 26 March 1947, J. Edgar Hoover testified before HUAC.

[Communism] stands for the destruction of our American form of government; it stands for the destruction of American democracy; it stands for the destruction of free enterprise; and it stands for the creation of a Soviet of the United States and ultimate world revolution...

What is important is the claim of the communists themselves that for every party member there are 10 others ready, willing and able to do the party's work. This is the greatest menace of communism. For these are the people who infiltrate and corrupt various spheres of American life. So rather than the size of the Communist Party, the way to weigh its true importance is by testing its influence, its ability to infiltrate...

THE HOLLYWOOD TEN

At a time when millions of people went to the cinema, there was a concern that communists would try to use the film industry to spread **propaganda**. From October 1947, HUAC called 41 writers, producers and directors for questioning about communism in **Hollywood**. They named 19 people as communists. When these 19 were ordered to appear before HUAC, ten refused to answer any questions and pleaded the **First Amendment** of the US Constitution. All ten were jailed for 1 year for **contempt** and were **blacklisted**. Most of them never worked in Hollywood again. The impact of investigating Hollywood was that it gave huge publicity to HUAC's work and increased anti-communist **hysteria**. It also had a big impact on Hollywood as film makers increased their production of anti-communist films.

ACTIVITY

1 Explain why J. Edgar Hoover thought HUAC would be useful in his fight against communism in the USA. Why would the investigation into Hollywood help with this?

2 Write a news headline and short report for a news website on either a) Hoover's testimony to HUAC (Source C) or b) the Hollywood Ten.

THE HISS CASE

Alger Hiss was a member of the State Department who had been an important adviser to President Roosevelt in the 1930s and during the Second World War. In 1948, during a HUAC hearing, Hiss was named as a member of a communist group. HUAC called him for questioning, but Hiss denied being a communist. Richard Nixon, a member of HUAC, insisted that Hiss had been leaking information to the Soviet Union, so Hiss went to trial in 1949. In January 1950, Hiss was sentenced to 5 years in prison for lying to the court. Although he was never convicted of spying, many people thought that he had been a spy, because he had been found guilty of something and sent to prison. Hiss had worked at the highest level of government, so this seemed to prove that Hoover was right – communist spies were everywhere, even in the highest offices in the land.

SOURCE E

Alger Hiss.

THE ROSENBERG CASE

In February 1950, Klaus Fuchs was arrested in Britain for passing on information to the Soviets on how to develop an atomic bomb. Fuchs confessed and was sentenced to 14 years in prison by the British court. He also named other spies, including David Greenglass. Greenglass was arrested in the USA and named his sister and brother-in-law, Ethel and Julius Rosenberg. The Rosenbergs denied all charges of spying at their trial in March 1951. The evidence against them at the time was weak (although some historians today are sure of their guilt), but they were found guilty and sentenced to death. They were executed on 19 June 1953.

THE IMPACT OF THE FBI'S AND HUAC'S WORK

Many in Hollywood defended the Hollywood Ten and the weak evidence used to send the Rosenbergs to their deaths led to large protests against their sentence. However, these were unusual reactions as most Americans seemed to believe their country was in the grip of a communist conspiracy. International events seemed to support this.

It was during Hiss' trial that news arrived of the Soviet Union's successful testing of an atomic bomb. This, combined with the Hiss case, meant that US fears of communists had never been greater. Congress passed the McCarran Internal Security Act in August 1950, which made all communist organisations register with the government.

The Rosenbergs were arrested after the outbreak of the Korean War. Some Americans believed in their **innocence**, but many more blamed the Rosenbergs for helping the Soviets to make atomic bombs. They thought this had led to North Korea's invasion of South Korea.

The number of **prosecutions** due to the work of the FBI and HUAC, and the public nature of HUAC's hearings combined with international events, made Americans worry that communists were everywhere. Many people believed that they were surrounded by communist spies looking to bring down the USA. People were suspicious of colleagues and neighbours and afraid of being accused themselves.

The McCarran Act was strengthened in 1952:
- Communists were not allowed US passports.
- Communists were not allowed to work in certain jobs.
- In an emergency, anyone suspected of '**subversion**' could be put in a **detention camp** without facing trial.

President Truman tried to stop the act but few agreed with him in Congress, so the act was passed. A major reason why so many members of Congress supported it was the activities of Senator Joseph McCarthy. '**McCarthyism**' had increased anti-communist hysteria even more.

KEY TERM

McCarthyism a term used to describe the anti-communist hysteria of the 1950s

EXAM-STYLE QUESTION

AO1   **AO2**

SKILLS PROBLEM SOLVING, REASONING, DECISION MAKING, ADAPTIVE LEARNING, INNOVATION

'The work of HUAC was the main reason for the Red Scare in the 1940s.'

How far do you agree? Explain your answer.

You may use the following in your answer:
- the work of HUAC
- the Cold War.

You **must** also use information of your own.   **(16 marks)**

HINT

For all questions like this one, you need to make a judgement on how far you agree with the statement and support your judgement with relevant points.

ACTIVITY

1 In pairs, discuss the impact of each of the factors below on people in the USA. How would each factor have made US citizens feel?
   - Federal Loyalty Boards
   - HUAC hearings on the threat posed by communism
   - the Hollywood Ten
   - Alger Hiss
   - Ethel and Julius Rosenberg.
2 Decide which of the factors listed in question 1 caused the biggest fear of communism in the USA. Give reasons for your choice.

1.4 THE ROLE OF MCCARTHY IN THE RED SCARE

LEARNING OBJECTIVES

- Understand the methods used by Joseph McCarthy
- Understand the growth of opposition to McCarthy
- Understand the overall impact of McCarthyism on the USA.

KEY TERMS

Republicans one of the two main political parties in the USA. Generally more right-wing than the Democrats

Democrats one of the two main political parties in the USA. Generally more left-wing than the Republicans

Joseph McCarthy became **Republican** senator for Wisconsin in 1946. His time as Senator was unimpressive but, after the Hiss trial, in February 1950, he made a speech claiming to have a list of 205 members of the Communist Party who worked in the US State Department. He then made several more speeches where the numbers varied until the number on the list was reduced to 57. Despite this, many senators and members of the public demanded an investigation. The Tydings Committee, made up of members of Congress, was set up to investigate but found that McCarthy's **accusations** were untrue. McCarthy's response was to call Senator Tydings 'un-American' and a communist **sympathiser**. Tydings was not re-elected later that year.

McCarthy had accessed the greatest fear of many Americans. His accusations also helped to explain why the Korean War, and the Cold War itself, was not going well for the USA. Therefore, despite the information found by the Committee, McCarthy still had the support of the Republican Party to carry out further investigations. In fact, the Republicans encouraged McCarthy as they realised he was popular and it gave them an issue on which to attack the **Democrats** in the 1952 election **campaign**. The Republicans won the election and most Democrats who had opposed McCarthy, like Tydings, lost their seats. The new president, Eisenhower, made McCarthy Chairman of the Government Committee on Operations of the Senate and, for the next 2 years, he led investigations into various government departments.

SOURCE F

Speech by Senator Joseph McCarthy, 9 February 1950.

The reason why we find ourselves in a position of impotency [powerlessness] is not because our only powerful potential enemy has sent men to invade our shores... but rather because of the traitorous actions of those who have been treated so well by this Nation. It has not been the less fortunate, or members of minority groups who have been traitorous to this Nation, but rather those who have had all the benefits that the wealthiest Nation on earth has had to offer... the finest homes, the finest college education and the finest jobs in government we can give.

This is glaringly true in the State Department. There the bright young men who are born with silver spoons in their mouths [i.e. wealth and privilege] are the ones who have been most traitorous... In my opinion the State Department, which is one of the most important government departments, is thoroughly infested with communists.

ACTIVITY

Read Source F. What do you think would have been the reaction of many Americans hearing this speech?

METHODS USED BY MCCARTHY

McCarthy held hearings, firstly in private and then in public. He used bullying and aggressive questioning of many suspected communists, especially attacking high-profile figures to gain more publicity. He tried to get them to confess. McCarthy gathered evidence, much of which was fed to him by the FBI. He also fabricated more evidence against those he accused. There were Democratic senators and journalists who spoke out against him, but he simply attacked them for being communist themselves or being 'soft on communism'.

Even though nobody accused by McCarthy was ever convicted of spying, he continued to win popular appeal. Thousands attended McCarthy's speeches and millions watched his television appearances. Just being called by McCarthy for questioning ended people's careers as others assumed they were guilty. It seemed like the whole of America was in the grip of McCarthyism.

EXTEND YOUR KNOWLEDGE

CHARLIE CHAPLIN
The comic movie actor is probably the most famous victim of the Red Scare. He was born in London but spent most of his life in the USA. The FBI and HUAC were suspicious of Chaplin because he had never applied for US citizenship and they thought they saw evidence of communist propaganda in his films. Chaplin denied being a communist when he appeared before HUAC in 1947, but his public reputation was damaged forever. When he visited Europe for a holiday in 1952, he was not allowed back into the USA. He spent the rest of his life in Switzerland.

MCCARTHY'S DOWNFALL

McCarthy's accusations grew increasingly extreme. He accused a popular war general – George Marshall – of helping the 'Communist drive for world domination' through the Marshall Plan (see page 7) and through his failure to prevent the communist victory in China. President Eisenhower, himself a popular war general, did nothing to support his friend because he was afraid of losing votes. **Opinion polls** in 1953 still showed that McCarthy's actions were popular with a majority of the American public, but that was to change, largely because of McCarthy's own actions.

By the autumn of 1953, McCarthy was leading a new Senate sub-committee on communist influence in the US Army. In Spring 1954, the Army–McCarthy hearings began. They were televised and, for the first time, the American public could see McCarthy at work. They were shocked by his bullying. The army itself fought back, finding evidence of McCarthy abusing his **privileges** as a member of Congress and sending this to reporters who were known to be critical of McCarthy. More anti-McCarthy material then appeared in the press. On 9 March, Ed Murrow broadcast an entire episode of his *See It Now* show on McCarthy, using video footage of McCarthy's speeches and actions to criticise him. Many historians credit this show as an important reason for McCarthy's downfall.

SOURCE G

Senator McCarthy showing a photograph during the Army–McCarthy hearings. It was supposed to provide evidence against the secretary of the army, but was later proved to have been faked.

▶ **Figure 1.4** Reasons for McCarthy's downfall

The army found and sent evidence of McCarthy's corruption to news reporters

The televised Army–McCarthy hearings meant the public saw McCarthy's bullying tactics

McCarthy's accusations became more extreme

Reasons for McCarthy's downfall

Nobody was ever convicted of spying based on McCarthy's work

The media produced an increasing number of anti-McCarthy articles and programmes

Cold War tensions had eased slightly after the ending of the Korean War in July 1953

On 2 December 1954, the Senate formally condemned Joseph McCarthy for 'improper conduct' by 67 votes to 22. McCarthy continued his work, but the media no longer wrote about it. He died from alcoholism in 1957.

ACTIVITY

1 Find and watch the *See It Now* episode and/or Army–McCarthy hearings on the internet. What does it show about the methods he used?
2 Create a mind map of McCarthy's methods.

SOURCE H

Journalist Edward Murrow on the television show, *See it Now*, CBS-TV, 9 March 1954.

The line between investigating and persecuting is a very fine one and the junior Senator from Wisconsin [McCarthy] has stepped over it repeatedly. His primary achievement has been in confusing the public mind, as between the internal and the external threats of Communism. We must remember always that accusation is not proof and that conviction depends upon evidence and due process of law. The actions of the junior Senator from Wisconsin have caused alarm and dismay amongst our allies abroad, and given considerable comfort to our enemies. And whose fault is that? Not really his. He didn't create this situation of fear; he merely exploited it – and rather successfully.

THE IMPACT OF MCCARTHYISM

McCarthyism had a direct impact on the thousands of people who lost their jobs or whose careers and lives were damaged by McCarthy's allegations. Companies and institutions were affected too. For example, the State Department lost hundreds of intelligent and talented people who may have steered US policies in another direction if they had remained.

However, the indirect impact of McCarthyism was bigger – hysteria was so common that almost everyone in America was affected by fears of the 'enemy within'. Thousands of ordinary Americans gave information to the FBI on people they suspected might be communists. People were seen as 'red' if they had **radical** or **socialist** ideas or even just different opinions. Trade unions were seen as communist organisations, which drastically reduced their influence and they rarely called for strikes. Fewer workers joined unions because they were afraid of being seen as communist. Many people stopped talking about politics or world events altogether for fear of being accused or seen as guilty. The Red Scare and McCarthyism also had a huge impact on politics as politicians rarely campaigned for **left-wing** policies and those who did were rarely elected. The USA was also damaged internationally because it was seen as intolerant of people with different ideas and more people became anti-American.

Some historians argue that the Red Scare lasted until the end of the Cold War in 1991. Certainly, although the mass hysteria of the McCarthy years cooled down, anxiety and fear of communism lasted long after 1954. US foreign policy remained firmly anti-communist and being seen as 'tough on communism' remained an important factor in presidential elections until the 1990s. However long it lasted, the Red Scare undoubtedly had a massive impact on America.

KEY TERMS

radical radical ideas are very new and different, and are against what most people think and believe

socialist relating to socialism, an economic and political system in which large industries are owned by the government and taxes are used to redistribute wealth

left-wing liberal, progressive views that believe in equality and government intervention to help enforce this

ACTIVITY

You should now have a completed timeline of all the international and domestic events of the Cold War and Red Scare, 1945–55. Identify 'hot spots', years where you think the Red Scare and McCarthyism reached particularly high levels.

EXTRACT B

From *United States 1917–2008 and Civil Rights 1865–1992*, published in 2008.

The damage done to ordinary people by the anti-Communist hysteria was massive. Hundreds lost their jobs due to the blacklists or for having been called before the Committee. Firms could be blacklisted as well as people, damaging their ability to conduct business. Between 1950 and 1952, 117 people were cited for contempt of Congress and jailed – more than in the whole of the previous century. A person did not need to be a Communist to suffer. Anyone who was radical could be accused, a problem which continued in the USA long after the hearings ended.

EXAM-STYLE QUESTION

A04

SKILLS ANALYSIS, INTERPRETATION, CREATIVITY

Study Extract B.

What impression does the author give about the impact of the Red Scare?

You **must** use Extract B to explain your answer. **(6 marks)**

EXAM TIP

For these questions, you need to firstly state what impression the author gives and then show how the author does this.

RECAP

RECALL QUIZ

1 What are the main differences between capitalism and communism?
2 Why did people in the USA fear communism?
3 Give two reasons why the Red Scare happened.
4 What do 'HUAC' and 'FBI' stand for?
5 Who were the following: J. Edgar Hoover, Joseph McCarthy, Alger Hiss, Ethel and Julius Rosenberg?
6 What were the Hollywood Ten imprisoned for?
7 What were the terms of the McCarran Act?
8 What methods were used by Joseph McCarthy to find communist spies in the US government?
9 Give three impacts of McCarthyism on the USA.
10 In what year did the following happen: the start of HUAC's investigation into communist spies; the trial of Hiss; the Rosenberg trial; the Soviet Union's testing of the atomic bomb?

CHECKPOINT

STRENGTHEN

S1 Explain why international events had a big impact on the Red Scare in the USA.
S2 Explain how the FBI and HUAC worked together to create anti-communist feelings and fears of communist spies in the USA.
S3 Describe the methods used by Joseph McCarthy to uncover communists in the US government and army.

CHALLENGE

C1 Were international or domestic events more important in creating the Red Scare?
C2 Why did so many people believe the accusations of Joseph McCarthy?
C3 Explain why anti-communist hysteria reached a peak in the 1950s.

SUMMARY

■ The USA was capitalist and the Soviet Union was communist. This meant there was distrust between them, which increased after the Second World War to become the Cold War.
■ During the years 1945–54, anti-communism in the USA increased as international events seemed to indicate that communists were trying to take over the world, including the USA.
■ The FBI and HUAC launched investigations and public hearings on the threat of communism. This led directly and indirectly to thousands of people losing their jobs.
■ Two famous spy cases – Alger Hiss and Ethel and Julius Rosenberg – seemed to prove to many Americans that there were communist spies everywhere, passing secrets, including information on how to create atomic bombs, to the Soviets.
■ Anti-communist hysteria reached a height in the early 1950s, in large part because of the work of Senator Joseph McCarthy, who used controversial methods to question suspected communists and fabricate evidence against them.
■ There was opposition to McCarthy and the Red Scare hysteria generally. This increased as McCarthy's accusations became more extreme, until he was discredited and the Red Scare cooled down. However, anti-communist feelings did not disappear completely.

EXAM GUIDANCE: PART (A) QUESTIONS

Study Extract A.

EXTRACT A

From an international history book, published in 2012.

McCarthy deliberately played on Red Scare fears. In speeches, interviews and TV appearances over several years, he stressed he had evidence to show there were communists in government (later in the army too). But when the Tydings Committee heard this evidence, it was very weak. The three Democratic members of the Committee… [called] the charges 'a fraud and a hoax, the most wicked campaign of half-truths and untruths in this country's history.'… McCarthy's reaction was to accuse Senator Tydings of having communist sympathies. He made more and more accusations, many of them now aimed at his personal and political enemies, including journalists who had spoken against him. McCarthy's accusations grew wilder, his evidence more obviously faked.

A04

SKILLS   ANALYSIS, INTERPRETATION, CREATIVITY

Question to be answered: What impression does the author give about Joseph McCarthy?

You must use Extract A to explain your answer.   (6 marks)

1   **Analysis Question 1: What is the question type testing?**
In this question you have to make an inference from what the extract says to show what impression the author set out to create. The key to analysing the extract is to understand that the author deliberately chooses how he/she writes. He/she will make a choice about what language to use, what tone to adopt and what content to include to create an impression.

2   **Analysis Question 2: What do I have to do to answer the question well?**
Obviously you have to read the extract carefully and work out what the author is trying to make you think. Has the author set out to give a positive or negative impression or has he/she set out to suggest that an event/policy or movement was significant/ineffective, successful/unsuccessful? The language and tone of the source will help you to see this. Are there any especially 'emotional' words? Has the author deliberately included things or left things out?

3   **Analysis Question 3: Are there any techniques I can use to make it very clear that I am doing what is needed to be successful?**
This is a 6-mark question and you need to make sure you leave enough time to answer the other two questions fully (they are worth 24 marks in total). So you want to answer this question as quickly as you can. A good way to do this is to answer the question straight away.

So why not begin with: 'The impression the author is trying to give about Joseph McCarthy is…'.

So now you have to prove it. A good way to do this is to say: 'I think this because of the language and tone…' Then quote Extract A to prove what you are saying about language and tone.

Another way is to say: 'I also think this is true because of the content the author has chosen…' Then quote Extract A to prove what you are saying about content choice. For example: 'The author creates a bad impression by not talking about the good things McCarthy did.'

Answer A

The impression the author is trying to give about Joseph McCarthy is that he is not trustworthy and made things up to accuse people of being communists. The author does this by using emotional language. Also, the author only includes negative information about McCarthy. The author quotes from people who were against what McCarthy was doing but doesn't quote anyone who supported McCarthy. There were plenty of people who supported McCarthy, especially to begin with, but once people saw him questioning people on television he started losing support as more people realised he was making stuff up.

What are the strengths and weaknesses of Answer A?

This answer starts well by saying what impression the author gives. However, the student doesn't support the answer with direct examples from the extract of 'emotional language' the author has chosen to use. It's good that the answer has included information on what the author has chosen to include and miss out but, again, this should be supported with concrete information, rather than the vague 'people who were against' McCarthy. The final sentence is totally unnecessary – you should only write about the extract itself and, by including extra information that isn't needed, the student has wasted valuable time.

Answer B

The impression the author is trying to give about Joseph McCarthy is that he is not trustworthy and is a liar who made things up to take advantage of the climate of the Red Scare. The author does this by using emotional language such as 'deliberately played on', 'weak' evidence, 'fraud and a hoax', 'accusations grew wilder, his evidence more obviously faked'. The other way in which the author gives the impression that McCarthy was an opportunist and untrustworthy is that they have chosen to include a very negative quote from the Democrats on the Tydings Committee, but nothing is included from people who supported McCarthy or approved of his actions.

What are the strengths and weaknesses of Answer B?

This is an excellent answer. It begins by stating the impression given and then supports this with details of the language used to give this impression as well as by highlighting what the author has chosen to include and leave out.

Challenge a friend

Use the Student Book to set a part (a) question for a friend. Then look at the answer. Does it do the following things?

☐ State a valid impression from the source
☐ Provide 3–4 lines explaining how language, tone and content choice prove this.

If it does, you can tell your friend that the answer is very good!

2. CIVIL RIGHTS IN THE 1950s

LEARNING OBJECTIVES

☐ Understand the impact of racial segregation and discrimination in the USA in the 1950s

☐ Understand efforts to challenge segregation and discrimination

☐ Understand the importance of the Civil Rights Act, 1957.

Before the American Civil War (1861–65), the whole way of life in the Southern states of America was based on slavery. One of the main reasons why the South went to war against the North was because the North wanted to end slavery. After the North's victory, black slaves were freed. By 1890, according to the US Constitution (see pages 3–4), African Americans were equal with white citizens. In practice, this was far from the case. African Americans found themselves facing racism, discrimination and often violence that continued well into the 20th century.

Although many civil rights groups that tried to improve equality existed before the 1950s, it was in this decade that the civil rights 'movement' really began, with a nationwide campaign and an increasing number of members. The focus of the 1950s was in two main areas: schools and public transport. In both areas, the campaigners met with some success.

2.1 SEGREGATION AND DISCRIMINATION

LEARNING OBJECTIVES

- ☐ Understand how races were segregated and African Americans were discriminated against throughout the USA by 1950
- ☐ Understand the differences between segregation in the North and the South of the USA
- ☐ Understand how and why the Supreme Court, Congress and the president appeared to accept segregation and discrimination.

SEGREGATION AND DISCRIMINATION

In 1950, most states had some segregation laws that meant black people and white people had to use different facilities. Segregation laws were most strictly enforced in the South, where they applied to almost all aspects of life. In these states, 'Jim Crow' laws meant African Americans attended separate schools, had to use separate areas in restaurants, libraries, cinemas and parks, and were also separated on public transport. Most of these laws had been passed by state legislatures and approved by state courts at the end of the 19th century.

In the North, there were fewer legal barriers to equality, but racism and discrimination meant that African Americans mostly lived separately from white people. Wages for black workers were generally half of what a white person earned for the same job and there was a higher rate of unemployment for African Americans. Therefore, black people could only afford to live in the poorest areas, where few white people were present. This meant facilities were often segregated without the need for laws.

According to the Constitution, all US citizens had the right to vote. However, in the 1950s very few African Americans in the South were able to vote.

SOURCE A

'Jim Crow' laws kept black and white people separate. Facilities for African Americans were almost always poorer in quality than those for white people.

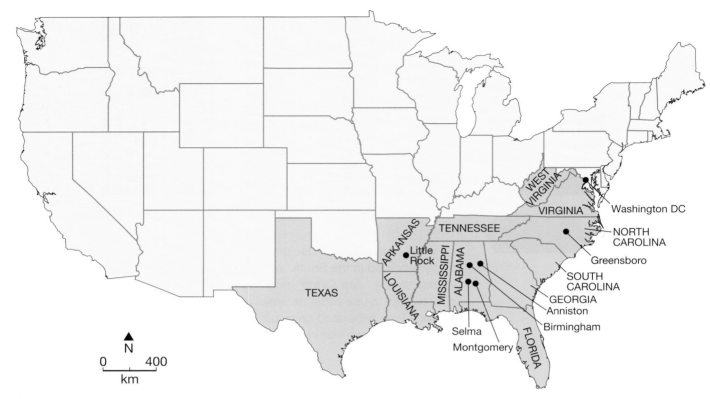

▲ Figure 2.1 The South of the USA (in green), where Jim Crow laws applied to most aspects of life

In order to vote, people had to register and most Southern states used methods to prevent black people from registering to vote including:

■ making people pass a difficult literacy test (testing their ability to read and write) – many African Americans had very little education, so their literacy levels were low and most did not even try to take the tests because they knew they would fail. (White people were exempted from these tests.)

■ making people pay a **poll tax** – most African Americans could not afford to pay this

■ using violence or threatening to use violence against African Americans who tried to register to vote.

As well as segregation and discrimination, African Americans often faced violence, particularly in the South. Black men suspected of crimes were frequently attacked by white mobs taking the law into their own hands. Although **lynchings** had declined by the 1950s, they were greatly feared by black communities. Police were sometimes racist themselves and did nothing to prevent attacks on African Americans, even taking part in them occasionally. White people suspected of attacking African Americans were usually found 'not guilty' by all-white, all-male juries.

KEY TERM

lynchings killings (usually hangings) done by a group, where the victim is suspected of a crime but has not been tried

THE ROLE OF THE FEDERAL GOVERNMENT IN MAINTAINING SEGREGATION

The Constitution of the United States guaranteed the equality of all American citizens, so why wasn't this the case with African Americans?

The three branches of government could have acted to enforce civil rights for African Americans, but this had not happened. Congress often needed the support of Southern politicians, who were either racist themselves or did not want to annoy racist voters in their states. Even a strong president frequently

SOURCE B

SOURCE B

From a speech given on 27 May 1954 by James Eastland, a senator for Mississippi and a supporter of 'Jim Crow' laws.

Separation promotes racial harmony. It permits [allows] each race to follow its own pursuits, and its own civilization. Segregation is not discrimination. Segregation is not a badge of racial inferiority, and that it is not is recognized by both races in the Southern States. In fact, segregation is desired and supported by the vast majority of the members of both races in the South, who dwell [live] side by side under harmonious conditions.

KEY TERM

precedent (legal) a ruling in a law case that is used by other courts when deciding similar cases

needed the support of Southern politicians for other policies, so presidents who may have wanted change did not act to improve civil rights. However, the Supreme Court was independent and did not rely on the support of either the president or Congress. It should have banned segregation laws because they were not constitutional, but this had not happened either. Instead, in 1896, the Federal Supreme Court had ruled in the *Plessy versus Ferguson* case that separate facilities were allowed *if* they were equal. They rarely were, but this legal **precedent** had been used time and time again when civil rights groups had tried to challenge segregation through the courts. Like other parts of government, the Supreme Court was influenced by the views and opinions of its judges and many of these were against civil rights for African Americans.

ACTIVITY

1 Write your own definitions of 'segregation' and 'discrimination'. Give three different examples of each.
2 According to James Eastland (Source B), what were the benefits of racial segregation? How popular do you think his views would have been?
3 In groups or as a class, discuss why the three branches of the US government had done little to give African Americans more civil rights.

2.2 *BROWN VERSUS TOPEKA* AND ITS IMPACT

LEARNING OBJECTIVES

☐ Understand the importance of the *Brown versus Topeka* case

☐ Understand why the Ku Klux Klan revived

☐ Understand the impact of the murder of Emmett Till on civil rights.

SOURCE C

A school for white children (left) and a school for black children (right), both in the small town of Farmville, Virginia, in the early 1950s.

ACTIVITY

Look at Source C in pairs. Describe the differences between the schools. Why do you think the schools were so different?

In many American states, not just in the South, white and black pupils had to attend separate schools. State government spending per pupil could be over four times more for white pupils, so this was an area where civil rights groups felt they could attack the 'separate but equal' principle of *Plessy versus Ferguson*. Therefore, from the 1940s, the civil rights campaign group the National Association for the Advancement of Colored People (NAACP) focused on challenging segregation in education through the law courts. This was a change of tactic as previously, the NAACP had tried to end segregation through Congress but had met with little success because it was opposed by many politicians (see page 34). To try and keep education segregated, some states began giving more money to African American schools to improve them. So, often, the NAACP's court cases met with little initial success. That changed in 1954.

BROWN VERSUS TOPEKA

In 1951, the parents of Linda Brown applied for her to attend the Summer Elementary school in the town of Topeka, Kansas, which was much closer to their house than the school she attended. The application was rejected by the Board of Education of Topeka on the grounds of race – Linda was black and Summer Elementary school was for white pupils only. Linda's parents, with the support of the NAACP, took their case to the local court, where it was rejected because of *Plessy versus Ferguson*. The NAACP persuaded Linda's parents to take their case to the Supreme Court, where it was combined with four other similar cases from around the country.

In December 1952, it was decided that a retrial of *Brown versus the Board of Education of Topeka* would be needed, as the judges had failed to reach a verdict and could not agree on a judgment. Before the retrial began, a new judge, Earl Warren, joined the Supreme Court and became Chief Justice. As the case restarted, NAACP lawyers led by Thurgood Marshall argued that separate schools were damaging African American children psychologically even if the schools were equal in terms of funding and facilities. On 17 May 1954, the Supreme Court ruled unanimously that school segregation was unconstitutional. Finally, the legal precedent of *Plessy versus Ferguson* had been broken and schools had to desegregate. A year after the *Brown* decision, a second Supreme Court ruling decided that school **desegregation** should happen 'with all deliberate speed', with states making 'a prompt and reasonable' start.

EXTEND YOUR KNOWLEDGE

THE 'DOLL' TEST

One of the main witnesses in the Brown case was Dr Kenneth Clark, a psychologist who used dolls in his work. He discovered that when black children were given four dolls, which were identical except for race, they preferred the white dolls. The children also gave the white dolls positive characteristics. He concluded that African American children developed a sense of inferiority, even self-hatred, due to segregation and discrimination.

EXTEND YOUR KNOWLEDGE

EARL WARREN

Earl Warren was also a Republican politician, who was appointed as Chief Justice by President Eisenhower. Later Eisenhower had become so annoyed by Warren's liberal judgments that he described the appointment as 'the biggest mistake I ever made'.

SOURCE D

Thurgood Marshall and his legal team pictured after the *Brown versus Topeka* decision.

ACTIVITY

1 Read Source E. Rewrite the paragraph using the simplest language you can. Make sure your version explains the reasons the Supreme Court made the decision it did.

2 Create a mind map of the consequences of the *Brown* decision.

3 What different reactions do you think people might have had to the *Brown* decision?

KEY TERMS

Deep South five states in the south east USA where segregation covered all aspects of life (Georgia, Alabama, South Carolina, Mississippi and Louisiana). Arkansas is also often included

integrate become part of a group or society, or help someone to do this

white supremacist someone who believes that white people are better than people of other races

Ku Klux Klan a racist organisation, started in 1865, that believes in the superiority of white, Protestant Christians

SOURCE E

Part of Chief Justice Earl Warren's statement giving the decision in the *Brown versus Board of Education of Topeka* case on 17 May 1954.

To separate children from others of similar age and qualifications solely because of their race generates a feeling of inferiority as to their status in the community that may affect their hearts and minds in a way unlikely to ever be undone. We conclude that in the field of public education the doctrine of "separate but equal" has no place. Separate educational facilities are inherently unequal. Therefore, we hold that the plaintiffs [people bringing the case] and others similarly situated are deprived of the equal protection of the laws guaranteed by the Fourteenth Amendment.

THE IMPORTANCE OF *BROWN VERSUS TOPEKA*

Despite the NAACP celebrations, *Brown versus Topeka* had a very limited immediate impact. Schools in towns and cities outside the **Deep South** started to **integrate**, but progress was fairly slow and did not always benefit African American pupils or teachers. Black pupils usually found integration very hard as they and their families faced anger and bad feeling, and their education suffered. Some African American teachers lost their jobs and many black schools that had provided a good education were closed. In some towns and cities, segregation became more extreme due to 'white flight', as white people left areas that had a large number of black residents. The negative impacts were at their worst in the Deep South, which saw an extreme backlash from white racists (see below).

However, the verdict was a great victory for the NAACP and brought an increased awareness of African American civil rights. Most importantly, it provided a new legal precedent and therefore led to many more legal cases and campaigns for desegregation. For the first time, the US political system, or at least the Supreme Court, seemed to be willing to support African American citizens. Therefore the case gave new hope to civil rights campaigners that the system could bring about change.

EXAM-STYLE QUESTION

A01   **A02**

Explain **two** effects of the *Brown versus Topeka* decision on the USA. **(8 marks)**

HINT

When answering a question on the effects of something, remember that 'effects' can be both positive and negative. Effects can also be immediate and more long term.

THE REVIVAL OF THE KU KLUX KLAN

In the Deep South, the day of the Supreme Court's decision in *Brown versus Topeka* became known as 'Black Monday'. Many white southerners were furious and determined to maintain segregation. The first White Citizens' Council was set up in Indianola, Mississippi for this purpose and was quickly followed by the establishment of many more WCCs across the South. They organised protests and **petitions** that put pressure on state authorities to resist integration. Many WCC members were also inspired to join the **white supremacist** group that black Americans feared above any other: the **Ku Klux Klan** (KKK).

Branches of the Ku Klux Klan reappeared all over the South and membership grew, although it never reached the level of the 1920s. The Klan once again held meetings encouraging racial hatred and put burning crosses in front of houses to frighten the people inside. Members wore their traditional long white robes and hoods as a disguise. Their targets were civil rights **protestors** and supporters, black or white. The initial growth of the Klan began after *Brown versus Topeka*, but the Klan continued to grow as more civil rights protests broke out across the USA. As the civil rights movement began to take off and meet with some success, the actions of the Klan became more extreme. They continued to use established methods such as beating, lynching and shooting victims; from January 1956, angered by the Montgomery Bus **Boycott** (see page 29), the KKK also began to use bombs. Historians believe Klan members were involved in most of the racial violence throughout the South in the 1950s and 1960s, even incidents that were not directly organised by the KKK.

KEY TERMS

protestors someone who takes part in a public activity such as a demonstration to show their opposition to something

boycott refuse to buy or use particular goods or services as a way of protesting

EXTEND YOUR KNOWLEDGE

FIRST KU KLUX KLAN BOMBING

It is believed that the first bomb used by the Ku Klux Klan was set off by the front door of the home of Martin Luther King in Montgomery on 30 January 1956. He was speaking at a meeting at the time but his wife and 10-week-old daughter were at home. Nobody was hurt but the house was quite badly damaged. A large angry mob of African Americans gathered outside the house. Some were armed and determined to get revenge for this attack, but King spoke to the crowd and persuaded them not to respond with violence.

SOURCE F

A Ku Klux Klan ceremony in Jacksonville, Florida, in 1950.

THE DEATH OF EMMETT TILL

The *Brown* verdict raised fears and tensions that led to increased violence against African Americans throughout the South. One terrible example of this was the murder of 14-year-old Emmett Till.

Till was from Chicago. As a northerner, he was used to discrimination and attended a segregated school, but he was not prepared for the extreme racism of the South when he visited relatives in the town of Money in Mississippi in the summer of 1955. On 24 August, Till boasted to a group of teenagers that he had a white girlfriend at home. His companions dared him to go into Bryant's Grocery and Meat Market shop and talk to the white owner's wife, Carolyn. The exact events inside the store will never be known but Till bought some bubble gum and Carolyn Bryant claimed he flirted and touched her. The teenagers with Till said that he whistled at her outside the store. Four days later, in the middle of the night, Till was taken from his great-uncle's house, by Carolyn's husband Roy and Roy's half-brother J.W. Milam. They beat him, shot him in the head and threw his body into the river, where it was found on 31 August.

The authorities in Mississippi wanted to bury Till quickly but his mother, Mamie Bradley, insisted that his body was sent back to her in Chicago. She hardly recognised her son because his face had been so badly beaten and therefore she left his coffin open so people could see what had been done to her child. Photographs of Till's body were published, so thousands of people saw him and many white people as well as African Americans were very shocked. The trial of Bryant and Milam was widely reported across the whole of America. It took just over an hour for the all-white, all-male **jury** to find the **defendants** 'not guilty'. Many Americans were angered by the lack of justice, especially when Bryant and Milam confessed to beating and killing Emmett Till in a magazine article they were paid for just a few months later. They were able to do this because, under US law, they could not be tried again for the same crime.

SOURCE G

From a statement released by the secretary of the NAACP after the murder of Emmett Till.

It would appear that the state of Mississippi has decided to maintain white supremacy by murdering children. The killers of the boy felt free to lynch him because there is in the entire state no restraining influence of decency, not in the state capital, among the daily newspapers, the clergy nor any segment of the so-called better citizens.

SOURCE H

From an American magazine on 3 October 1955, reporting on the trial of Bryant and Milam.

The white people in the region raised a defense fund approaching $10,000 for defendants Bryant and Milam. They hired five local lawyers, who produced expert witnesses — including a doctor and an embalmer — to testify that the bloated, decomposing body had been in the river for at least ten days, and therefore could not have been Emmett Till. Sheriff Strider took the stand for the defense and said the same thing: "If it had been one of my own boys, I couldn't have identified it." In most of the U.S., this conflict over the identity of the body could have been resolved by basic police work.

ACTIVITY

1 How do you think a) African Americans and b) white residents of Mississippi would have reacted to Source G?
2 Read Source H carefully. What was the role of a) the police and b) white supporters of Bryant and Milam in getting them acquitted?

The publicity generated after the murder of Emmett Till inspired many protests, such as this one in Sharp Street Church, Baltimore in September 1955.

THE IMPACT OF EMMETT TILL'S DEATH

The killing of an African American and his murderers' **acquittal** was not unusual at this time in the South. It was the publicity that this case received that made it different. It was to have two important consequences.

1 Many white Americans in the North saw for the first time the extreme racism that African Americans in the South were suffering. This brought an increased awareness of the problems African Americans faced.

2 It motivated many African Americans to take a more active role to bring about change. Many African Americans of the same age identified with Emmett Till and went on to join the huge civil rights protests of the 1960s. Indeed, some historians believe that what happened to Emmett Till was the **catalyst** for the civil rights movement.

EXAM-STYLE QUESTION

A01   **A02**

SKILLS PROBLEM SOLVING, REASONING, DECISION MAKING, ADAPTIVE LEARNING, INNOVATION

'The main effect of the *Brown versus Topeka* decision on African Americans was the increase in violence against them.'

How far do you agree? Explain your answer.

You may use the following in your answer:
- *Brown versus Topeka*
- the murder of Emmett Till.

You **must** also use information of your own. **(16 marks)**

HINT

In questions which ask 'how far you agree' with a statement you will be given two bullet points. These are to help you but you do not have to use them if you do not want to. You **must** use your own information whether you use the prompts or not.

2.3 THE MONTGOMERY BUS BOYCOTT AND ITS IMPACT

LEARNING OBJECTIVES

- Understand the key events of the Montgomery Bus Boycott
- Understand the degree of support for the boycott
- Understand the significance of the boycott.

WHAT CAUSED THE BOYCOTT?

On 1 December 1955, Rosa Parks travelled home from work on a bus in Montgomery, Alabama. As in most places in the South, buses in Montgomery were segregated. Parks sat in the first row for 'colored' people. When more people got on the bus, one white man did not have a seat. Rosa and the other black people in her row were told by the bus driver to stand so the white man could sit down. The whole row had to stand as mixed race rows were not allowed. The others did stand up but Rosa refused. The driver stopped the bus and called the police, who arrested Rosa.

The Women's Political Council in Montgomery had been fighting discrimination on buses since 1950. They wanted to improve the service, particularly for African American women who were routinely bullied by drivers, and had warned Mayor Gayle that there would be a boycott if the bus service did not improve. Rosa Parks was not the first African American to be arrested for refusing to comply with bus segregation laws. However, after she was arrested, her case was chosen as the one to start a boycott. Rosa was highly respectable and was already involved in civil rights through being secretary of the NAACP in Montgomery. The WPC called for all African Americans to boycott buses on 5 December – the day of Rosa Parks' trial. Church and college groups helped to publicise the boycott and it was a huge success. Montgomery's buses were nearly empty: approximately 70 per cent of all bus passengers were African American, and around 90 per cent of African Americans did not use the buses that day. Civil rights **activists** realised they had found a useful method that could bring about change.

SOURCE J

Rosa Parks speaking about what happened on 1 December 1955, 3 months after Emmett Till's death.

I thought about Emmett Till, and when the bus driver ordered me to move to the back, I just couldn't move.

SOURCE K

From a leaflet made by Jo Ann Robinson, President of the Women's Political Council, on 1 December 1955.

Another Negro woman has been arrested and thrown into jail because she refused to get up out of her seat on the bus for a white person to sit down. It is the second time since the Claudette Colvin case that a Negro woman has been arrested for the same thing. This has to be stopped.

Negroes have rights, too, for if Negroes did not ride the buses, they could not operate. Three-fourths of the riders are Negroes, yet we are arrested, or have to stand over empty seats. If we do not do something to stop these arrests, they will continue. The next time it may be you, or your daughter, or mother.

This woman's case will come up on Monday. We are, therefore, asking every Negro to stay off the buses Monday in protest of the arrest and trial. Don't ride the bus to work, to town, to school, or anywhere else on Monday.

You can afford to stay out of school for one day if you have no other way to go except by bus. You can also afford to stay out of town for one day. If you work, take a cab, or walk. But please, children and grown-ups, don't ride the bus at all on Monday. Please stay off the buses.

ACTIVITY

1 Why would Emmett Till have been a reason for Rosa Parks to refuse to move as the bus driver asked (Source J)?
2 Discuss reasons why so many of the people who used the buses in Montgomery were African American.
3 How would Source K have inspired African Americans in Montgomery to boycott the buses on 5 December?

THE BOYCOTT CONTINUED

SOURCE L

A bus in Montgomery during the boycott. The lack of African American passengers meant the bus company lost a lot of money during the boycott.

On the evening of 5 December, a large group gathered at Holt Street Baptist Church. They set up the Montgomery Improvement Association, which aimed to improve integration throughout Montgomery – beginning with its buses. A local minister, Martin Luther King, was chosen as its chairman. The MIA decided to continue the boycott until the bus company agreed to their demands:

■ Drivers should treat all African American passengers with respect.

■ Black drivers should be used for routes with mostly black passengers.

■ African Americans should not have to leave their seats in the 'colored' section of the bus so white people could sit down.

King and other leaders of the MIA met with those who ran the bus company on 8 December. They refused all of the MIA's demands. With **hindsight** this seems like a foolish decision by the bus company, as the boycott continued for 381 days, causing serious financial harm to the company. It also led to the demands of the MIA hardening: it began to demand a complete end to segregation.

MAINTAINING THE BOYCOTT

The MIA realised that the boycott would be very difficult for many people to maintain without help because of distance, carrying heavy items or being physically unable to walk far. It initially arranged for black taxi companies to charge lower fares and for those with cars to give others lifts. Some white car owners, often their employers, also gave African Americans lifts. Two of these options soon became unavailable as the white community put pressure on those who had been giving lifts to black people to stop doing so and an old law was restored that raised minimum taxi fares to make them too expensive for most African Americans. The black community needed another solution.

The MIA began organising a car-pooling system, where people shared cars and many churches bought cars to be used. It developed pick up and drop off points and routes around the city to make sure there was an effective method of transporting people. The support of several churches in Montgomery was essential for the boycott's success. Most African Americans attended church, so this was a great place to create support for the boycott and encourage people to keep going. Ministers were crucial in this. The churches provided meeting places for planning and discussion and raised money for shared cars. They even bought people shoes, as all that walking meant that people were wearing their shoes out very quickly! The role of ministers and churches became vital in the civil rights movement.

Despite the various forms of help, the boycotters still faced problems from many of the furious white citizens of Montgomery.

- They were verbally and physically **harassed** while waiting for cars to arrive.
- Drivers of shared cars were frequently arrested for very minor driving offences.
- Laws that prevented crowds gathering were used to arrest groups of people waiting for shared cars.

Violence reached new levels on 30 January when Martin Luther King's house was bombed (see Extend box, page 26). This was followed by bombings of churches and the houses of other leaders.

EXTRACT A

From an African American history website.

The MIA was the first of its kind, an organization based in the Deep South that specifically adopted a direct action tactic (a bus boycott) to challenge racial discrimination. The MIA was also the first predominately black civil rights organization to operate independently of the National Association for the Advancement of Colored People (NAACP).

Although the MIA was not the catalyst to the Montgomery bus boycott, it played a significant role in the success of the protest and the desegregation of the buses, a year later. The MIA took responsibility for maintaining the boycott and the morale of the protesters and was in charge of providing alternative transportation for those who refused to ride the buses. Its car pools formed an effective means for the most impoverished black employees who could not walk to work to continue their employment.

EXAM-STYLE QUESTION

A04

SKILLS SKILLS ANALYSIS, INTERPRETATION, CREATIVITY

Study Extract A.

What impression does the author give about the Montgomery Improvement Association?

You **must** use Extract A to explain your answer. **(6 marks)**

HINT

This question is testing how you analyse and evaluate a historical interpretation. Therefore, you only need to focus on the extract in your answer – your own knowledge should be used to consider what the author has said (or deliberately not said).

THE MOVE TO COMPLETE INTEGRATION

Due to the support of the car pools and inspiring speeches given by King, the boycotters did not give up and their determination to succeed seemed to increase. As the boycott continued, the media became more interested and media coverage increased, raising awareness of the problems of segregation and attracting support for the cause. The NAACP stepped in and decided to challenge the issue of segregated transport in court as it had done with segregated education. On 1 February 1956, the case of *Browder versus Gayle* began in the local court. This case argued that segregation of the buses was a violation of the Fourteenth Amendment (which gave equal protection of the law to all American citizens). This led the MIA to change their approach and demand total desegregation of the buses as well.

On 22 February, around 90 leading members of the MIA, including King and Parks, were arrested for 'disrupting lawful business'. They were jailed until their trial on 19 March. All were found guilty and some had to pay fines. However, the trial gave the MIA an opportunity to show evidence of the abuses of white bus drivers, which gave the trial and the boycott even more publicity. It also attracted funding for the MIA as people from all over the USA sent donations to enable the boycott to continue.

On 5 June, the three judges in the *Browder versus Gayle* case ruled by two to one that buses should be desegregated because the *Brown versus Topeka* decision should be applied to transport as well as education. The bus company, supported by White Citizens' Councils, appealed to the Supreme Court, but lost a first appeal on 13 November. The company tried again but lost the second appeal on 17 December. The Supreme Court agreed that buses should be desegregated. The MIA ended the boycott and, on 20 December 1956, African Americans returned to the buses. They could now sit wherever they wanted to.

ACTIVITY

1 Create a poster or leaflet that could have been used to help maintain the morale of the black community during the Montgomery Bus Boycott.
2 a Make a mind map of reasons why the boycott was successful.
  b Which reason do you think was the most important for the boycott's success? Explain why.

EXTRACT B

From a school textbook, published in 2010.

The Montgomery Bus Boycott was a turning point in the civil rights movement. Black protestors saw that by acting together they had significant economic power.

During the boycott, the bus company's revenue went down by 65%. Local businesses lost custom. It was estimated that the boycott caused losses of about $1 million. Therefore white businessmen became anxious to resolve the dispute.

Success was also due to solidarity in the black community. People walked together or shared cars and taxis to get to work… They resisted intimidation and tried to avoid violence. Crucially, there wasn't a way of rigging the system: the bus companies needed black passengers.

THE SIGNIFICANCE OF THE MONTGOMERY BUS BOYCOTT

The Montgomery Bus Boycott can be regarded as very successful. Afterwards, buses in Montgomery were integrated, seating was on a first-come first-served basis rather than by race and bus drivers no longer ordered African Americans to make room for white passengers. After the boycott, some other places began to integrate public transport. The real significance of the boycott was that it provided an example of a form of protest that worked. This inspired more civil rights campaigns, such as the Tallahassee Bus Boycott of 1956–58. Events after *Brown versus Topeka* had proved that changing the law was not enough to achieve equality. The bus boycott showed that, when large numbers of African Americans took direct action, this brought about real change. It demonstrated the effectiveness of non-violence in gaining support for civil rights and attracting publicity. Moreover, it showed how effectively African Americans could organise themselves and demonstrated the power of churches in bringing people together for a cause. Perhaps its most lasting impact, however, was that it brought to public attention the work of Martin Luther King. He would become really important in raising awareness of civil rights and attracting supporters to the campaigns.

Civil rights leaders on one of the first integrated bus rides in Montgomery, Alabama, 21 December 1956.

EXTEND YOUR KNOWLEDGE

GLENN SMILEY

Glenn Smiley was a minister who became committed to racial equality. He first used the theory of non-violent protest to try and integrate tearooms in Los Angeles department stores in the late 1940s. Smiley was sent to Montgomery after the boycott began, to help advise the leaders of the protest. He was impressed with Martin Luther King and together they developed guidelines for the non-violent approach that King would use in all the protests he led. Smiley asked King if he could be the first white person to sit beside him on a bus on their first integrated bus ride, shown in Source M.

The significance was not all positive, as the boycott only led to change in one small area. Other facilities in Montgomery remained segregated for many years afterwards. Furthermore, membership numbers for racist groups rose and the bus boycott marked an increase in violence against African American communities. There was a serious backlash after 20 December when bus integration began. Hooded patrols of the Ku Klux Klan drove around Montgomery trying to intimidate and sometimes attacking African American residents. Some integrated bus passengers were attacked by snipers and there was a wave of bombings of African American churches and the homes of civil rights leaders. This led to a complete suspension of bus services for a few weeks but things did eventually calm down.

EXAM-STYLE QUESTION

A01   **A02**

SKILLS   PROBLEM SOLVING, REASONING, DECISION MAKING, ADAPTIVE LEARNING, INNOVATION

'The Montgomery Bus Boycott was the most successful civil rights event of the 1950s.'

How far do you agree? Explain your answer.

You may use the following in your answer:
- the Montgomery Bus Boycott
- *Brown versus Topeka*.

You **must** also use information of your own.   (16 marks)

HINT

You need to show your knowledge of the events and analyse their success to answer this question well.

2.4 THE 1957 CIVIL RIGHTS ACT

LEARNING OBJECTIVES

☐ Understand the events leading to the 1957 Civil Rights Act

☐ Understand opposition to the 1957 Civil Rights Act

☐ Understand the significance of the 1957 Civil Rights Act.

KEY TERMS

Dixiecrats a separate, pro-segregation political party formed by the Southern Democrats in 1948

filibuster a tactic used in Congress to stop a vote on a bill; the most common filibuster is to talk until the time limit for the debate is reached

By 1957, one of the three parts of Federal government – the Supreme Court – had taken action on African American civil rights in the fields of education and public transport. However, the other two parts of government – the president and Congress – had yet to act. The Democratic President Truman had attempted to get a civil rights **bill** passed in 1948, but it had been blocked by Republicans (on party grounds) and **Dixiecrats** (who were strongly pro-segregation). When Truman was replaced by Republican President Eisenhower in 1952, it was hoped that he would push his own civil rights bill through Congress.

Eisenhower declared himself to be in support of African American civil rights, but seemed unwilling to act. Like many politicians, he believed that changing the law would not really work until people's attitudes towards African Americans changed. He was also aware of how strongly people valued 'states' rights' and did not want Federal government to interfere in what was seen as states' affairs, However, the achievements of *Brown versus Topeka* and the Montgomery Bus Boycott, and the extreme violent reactions to them, put pressure on the president and Congress for a Federal law to help African Americans achieve civil rights.

A bill was introduced in 1956, but was not passed because of Southern **resistance**. Strom Thurmond, a leading Dixiecrat, **filibustered** for an astonishing 24 hours and 18 minutes, so the bill took longer than the time allowed and was rejected. Eisenhower's administration tried again in 1957 with a revised version. Again, Dixiecrats tried to delay and destroy the bill but, due partly to the work of Lyndon Johnson (see pages 55–58), the Democrats' leader in the Senate, a weakened version of the bill was finally passed.

President Eisenhower signed the Civil Rights Act on 9 September 1957. The act focused on trying to improve the number of African American voters by:
■ setting up the US Commission on Civil Rights, which began investigating how African Americans were prevented from voting in different places
■ allowing Federal courts to prosecute states who tried to prevent people from voting.

THE SIGNIFICANCE OF THE 1957 CIVIL RIGHTS ACT

The Civil Rights Act had little immediate impact. Although Federal courts could prosecute states, juries were often opposed to increasing civil rights, so they were likely to reach 'not guilty' verdicts. Therefore, the act was not very significant in improving civil rights for African Americans. However, it was a hugely important first step – it was the first time in 82 years that the Federal government had acted to try to improve the civil rights of African Americans

President Eisenhower (fourth from left) meeting civil rights leaders at the White House in June 1958.

Prepare a presentation on the progress in African American civil rights during the 1950s. Was much actual progress made? Include reasons why progress was so slow and difficult.

in law. This showed that Congress was at last willing to do something. Eisenhower thought that the act would satisfy civil rights campaigners and stop the protests that were so damaging to the USA's international reputation. The opposite happened! Civil rights activists were disappointed that the act did not go as far as they wanted, and they became even more determined to press for further **reform**.

Perhaps the most important result of the ineffective Civil Rights Act of 1957 was that Congress passed another Civil Rights Act in 1960. This act was important because it introduced Federal inspections of the process used by state governors to register voters and penalties for those states found to be obstructing people from registering to vote. However, the two acts only improved the number of African Americans registering to vote by 3 per cent.

▼ **Figure 2.2** The influence of the Supreme Court and Congress on civil rights in the 1950s

An important first step by Congress in trying to improve civil rights for African Americans through changing the law

Acknowledged that many African Americans were unable to vote and that something should be done about this

The 1957 Civil Rights Act was the first time that Congress had tried to improve civil rights for African Americans in the 20th century

Had little direct impact in improving civil rights and therefore showed the limited effect of Supreme Court action on its own

Encouraged civil rights campaigners to push for further laws which would have an impact – was followed by another Civil Rights Act in 1960

The influence of the Supreme Court and Congress on civil rights in the 1950s

The decision in Browder versus Gayle was upheld by the Supreme Court which meant that it was illegal to segregate public transport

Brown versus Topeka – the first time the Supreme Court acknowledged that 'separate was not equal' and that schools should be desegregated

Led to an increase in violence against African Americans

Only affected transport, just one small area of African Americans' lives

Had little immediate impact and it was very difficult to enforce

Where schools did desegregate this often did not benefit African American pupils whose education suffered from the hostility they faced

Proved that Supreme Court action was more successful when it was done at the same time as other measures, in this case the Montgomery Bus Boycott

Led to integration of public transport firstly in Montgomery, then gradually across the USA

Provided a new legal precedent – led to many more cases for desegregation in other areas

Led to White Citizens Councils and increased violence against African Americans

Showed civil rights campaigners that the US Supreme Court was prepared to help African Americans

2.5 ENFORCING SCHOOL DESEGREGATION

LEARNING OBJECTIVES

- Understand why desegregation was an issue in the Southern states of the USA
- Understand the events at Little Rock in 1957
- Understand the significance of events at Little Rock.

Although it took time for schools all over the USA to start the process of desegregating, by 1957 not one school in the Deep South had been integrated. This was largely because the authorities in these states, supported by white public opinion, made moves to prevent it. Southern senators opposed the *Brown* decision by signing the Southern Manifesto, which stated that *Brown* was an abuse of the Supreme Court's power. State governors supported White Citizens' Councils and some closed public schools completely to prevent integration. President Eisenhower did nothing to enforce the Supreme Court's decision that schools must desegregate but events at Little Rock in 1957 finally forced him to act.

EVENTS AT LITTLE ROCK IN 1957

SOURCE O

This photo of Elizabeth Eckford, aged 15, walking to school surrounded by angry, screaming white women is one of the most famous from the civil rights movement. The NAACP had organised for the nine students to arrive together but Eckford's family did not have a telephone, and so she did not get the message and had to brave the crowd alone.

A Federal Court had ruled that the all-white Central High School in Little Rock, Arkansas, must start integration in 1957, against the wishes of most of the white community and Arkansas' governor, Orval Faubus. To obey, the school accepted applications from African Americans and selected 25 students to start school in September 1957. These teenagers and their families were the victims of many threats from their white neighbours, so only nine students still wanted to join the school when the time came. They would become known as the Little Rock Nine.

To prevent the nine students enrolling, Governor Faubus announced on television the day before that he had ordered state troops to stop the students entering the school for their own protection. He knew publicising a school's integration in this way would cause a reaction. On the first day of school on 4 September, the nine African American students arrived and were surrounded by an angry mob of white people screaming abuse at them. The state troops prevented them entering the school so they had to go home. All this was captured by reporters and photographers and shown all over the world, as well as throughout the USA.

EXTEND YOUR KNOWLEDGE

HAZEL BRYAN
The girl with her mouth wide open, screaming at Elizabeth Eckford, in Source O was 15-year-old Hazel Bryan. After the photograph was published around the world, Bryan became almost as well-known as Eckford. She received hate mail and her parents took her out of the Central High School completely. Years later, Bryan became a peace activist and social worker, who spent much time trying to help African Americans. Her racist ideas and opinions had been completely changed.

SOURCE P

Elizabeth Eckford remembers the events of 4 September 1957.

I walked up to the guard who had let the white students in... When I tried to squeeze past him, he raised his bayonet and then the other guards moved in and raised their bayonets... I was very frightened and didn't know what to do. I turned around and the crowd came toward me... Somebody started yelling, 'Lynch her! Lynch her!' I tried to see a friendly face somewhere in the mob... I looked into the face of an old woman and it seemed a kind face, but when I looked at her again she spat on me. They came closer, shouting, 'No n***** bitch is going to get in our school.'

SOURCE Q

From a televised address by President Eisenhower on 24 September 1957.

Mob rule cannot be allowed to override the decision of our courts... At a time when we face grave [serious] situations abroad because of the hatred that Communism bears toward a system of government based on human rights, it would be difficult to exaggerate the harm that is being done... Our enemies are gloating over this incident... We are portrayed as a violator of [breaking] those standards which the people of the world united to proclaim in the Charter of the United Nations.

In the following days, the troops and angry crowds continued to prevent the Little Rock Nine from entering the school. On 12 September, President Eisenhower met with Governor Faubus to try to persuade him to let the students go to school. A Federal judge began legal proceedings against the governor and ordered the troops to be removed. The police took over and managed to successfully accompany the students into the school on 23 September. However, this caused a riot outside, so the students were sent home yet again. All of this was broadcast to a shocked world and it was probably media pressure that finally forced the president to act. Eisenhower signed a presidential order that sent 1,200 Federal troops to Little Rock and put them in charge of the local state troops, who would protect the African American students. On 25 September, 3 weeks after term had started, the Little Rock Nine were at last able to go to classes.

For the whole year, the Little Rock Nine were protected by the army, but they and their families continued to experience harassment and even violence. In September 1958, Governor Faubus closed all high schools in Little Rock while the state court fought the Supreme Court over desegregation. A public vote confirmed that 72 per cent of Little Rock's citizens were against integrating schools, but the Supreme Court stood by the *Brown* decision and schools were forced to re-open in August 1959 and continue integrating. There were still protests and violence, although much less than before. However, it was not until the 1970s that there was a significant level of school integration in Little Rock.

ACTIVITY

1 What can you learn about attitudes in the USA from Source O?
2 Elizabeth Eckford faced terrible abuse when she tried to enter Little Rock High School. Why do you think she kept returning until she was allowed into the school?
3 Write a paragraph explaining why the president intervened during events at Little Rock.

THE SIGNIFICANCE OF EVENTS AT LITTLE ROCK

This was the only occasion where the president directly intervened to enforce the Supreme Court's decision that high schools should be integrated. Nevertheless, it did show that the Federal government could successfully overrule state governments even if events had to reach extreme levels for this to happen. As with the Emmett Till murder, it was the publicity generated by the events at Little Rock that caused the most significant impact, as millions of

US citizens saw another example of extreme racism in the South. This time the publicity was international, which damaged the USA's reputation and made the country look **hypocritical** for criticising other countries' civil rights. Little Rock showed civil rights campaigners that winning battles in the Supreme Court would not be enough to end segregation. They would need to take other action as well. It also demonstrated that media coverage was essential for bringing about change.

It was not just at Little Rock that African American students faced angry crowds when they tried to go to schools that had previously been all-white. Throughout the South, many pupils had to be accompanied by police or state troops. Once inside school, African American pupils were frequently insulted or not spoken to by white pupils. Many felt their education suffered.

EXTRACT C

From a history of the United States of America.

But, of course, the process of dismantling segregation could not be plain sailing. For one thing, to attack it in the schools was to attack it everywhere. The structure of white supremacy tottered [shook]. The Deep South rose in wrath [anger] and came together in fear. It resolved to evade or defeat this decision as it had with so many others, and in carrying out this resolution it had, to start with, considerable success. *Brown* v. [versus] *Board of Education* turned out to be only the first blow in the new battle in the long, long war. As a result of the great decision it was possible for Southern black schoolchildren and college-age students to claim admission to formerly all-white institutions; but making good that claim was another matter.

The events of the mid-1950s – the campaigns for equality in education and the Montgomery Bus Boycott – had won some small victories and inspired more civil rights protests in different parts of the USA. By the end of the decade, there were signs that a civil rights movement, rather than a few separate events, was building. However, there was still a long way to go before segregation in all areas would end and African Americans would achieve equal civil rights to white Americans.

ACTIVITY

1 Create a diagram or table showing the successes and failures of the civil rights campaigns on education in the 1950s.
2 President Eisenhower believed that changing the law to enforce integration would do more harm than good. Did events at Little Rock prove that he was right?

EXAM-STYLE QUESTION

A01 **A02**

Explain **two** effects of the events at Little Rock in September 1957 on the USA.
(8 marks)

HINT

In this type of question, you need to demonstrate your knowledge of the events and show an understanding of the consequences.

RECAP

RECALL QUIZ

1 What were 'Jim Crow' laws?
2 What was the name of the 1896 court case where it was ruled that 'separate but equal' facilities were allowed?
3 What do the letters NAACP stand for?
4 What was the decision in the *Brown versus Topeka* case?
5 Give three examples of how white extremists reacted to growing calls for improved civil rights for African Americans.
6 Who was Emmett Till?
7 Who was US president, 1953–61?
8 When did the Little Rock Nine try to join the Central High School in Little Rock?
9 How did the African American community of Montgomery manage not to use buses for 381 days?
10 What was the decision in the *Browder versus Gayle* case?

CHECKPOINT

STRENGTHEN

S1 Explain why *Brown versus Topeka* was significant in improving African American civil rights.
S2 Why do some historians consider the death of Emmett Till to be so important for the civil rights movement?
S3 Explain why the Montgomery Bus Boycott was successful in ending bus segregation in Montgomery.

CHALLENGE

C1 Explain why the Federal government took so long to act to improve civil rights.
C2 Which events of the 1950s helped to create publicity for the civil rights movement? Why was publicity so important in bringing about change?
C3 Which out of *Brown versus Topeka*, the Montgomery Bus Boycott and the Little Rock Nine had the greatest positive impact on African Americans?

SUMMARY

- In the 1950s, African Americans experienced much racism, discrimination and segregation. This was more extreme in the Southern states.
- In the *Brown versus Topeka* court case, the Supreme Court found that segregated schools were unconstitutional and ordered schools to start accepting people of all races.
- The *Brown* case provoked an extreme reaction from some Southern white people.
- Emmett Till was beaten and murdered for whistling at a white woman in 1955.
- The Montgomery Bus Boycott lasted for 381 days until segregation on buses was found to be illegal by the Supreme Court.
- The Civil Rights Act of 1957 had a very limited impact on improving African American civil rights, but it did at least show that Congress was willing to act.
- The Little Rock Nine attended Central High School in Little Rock after President Eisenhower finally intervened.

EXAM GUIDANCE: PART (B) QUESTIONS

A01   **A02**

Question to be answered: Describe two effects on the USA of the death of Emmett Till.

(8 marks)

1 **Analysis Question 1: What is the question type testing?**
In this question you have to demonstrate that you have knowledge and understanding of the key features and characteristics of the period studied. You also have to consider historical events to work out what effects they had. In this particular case, you must show knowledge and understanding of the death of Emmett Till and the events caused by his death.

2 **Analysis Question 2: What do I have to do to answer the question well?**
Obviously you have to write about the death of Emmett Till! But don't simply write everything you know. You have to write about two effects. What are effects? They are things that the subject you are given caused to happen. The key to explaining the effects of an event is to explain the link between the event and an outcome. So, for example, an effect of you doing a lot of revision should be that you can answer the questions in the exam better. You would explain this by emphasising that you know more facts, you have to spend less time trying to remember things, you have looked at more examples of how to answer questions, and so on.

3 **Analysis Question 3: Are there any techniques I can use to make it very clear that I am doing what is needed to be successful?**
This is an 8-mark question and you need to make sure you leave enough time to answer the other two questions fully (they are worth 22 marks in total). Remember, you are not writing an essay here. You are providing two effects and enough historical detail to explain why the event had these effects.

Therefore, you need to get straight in to writing your answer.

The question asks for two effects, so it's a good idea to write two paragraphs and to begin each paragraph with a phrase like: 'One effect was…', 'Another effect was…'. You should also try to use phrases such as: 'this led to'; 'as a result of this'; 'this brought about'; 'this resulted in'. This will help to show that you are focusing on effects.

The word 'explain' is important because it tells you that you have to do more than just state what the effect was. You need to use your knowledge of the period to explain how the effect led to the outcome. So 'this led to…' states an effect, but 'this led to… because at this time…' is moving towards an explanation.

You cannot get more than 4 marks if you explain only one effect. However, you are required to explain only two effects and you will not gain credit for a third. If you do write about more than two, your better two will be credited and the third will be disregarded.

Answer A

Emmett Till's death shocked and horrified many Americans. This was because his mother kept the lid open on his coffin so people saw how badly he had been attacked as photos were published in many newspapers.

What are the strengths and weaknesses of Answer A?

This answer is quite weak. It identifies only one effect (that many Americans were shocked by Till's death), rather than two. It then supports this one effect with quite limited detail. The answer needs to show why many Americans were so shocked and what impact this had – Till's horrible death and the actions of his mother highlighted the extreme racism of the South, which many Americans, particularly in the North, were unaware of. This increased sympathy for civil rights protests.

Answer B

One effect of Emmett Till's death was that it shocked and horrified many Americans who previously did not realise how racist some people in the South were and the treatment that African Americans were subjected to there. This was because Till's mother, Mamie Bradley, insisted that his coffin was left open so people could see how badly her son had been beaten. His body was photographed and published in newspapers so many people saw it. This increased awareness of racism and brought more support for civil rights protests.

Another effect of Till's death was that it angered many African Americans, and motivated them to join protests and do more to improve African American civil rights. Some people even believe that Till's death was the catalyst for the civil rights movement. This was not just because of the horrible way he was killed for little reason, but because he was so young. Some of the people who supported Rosa Parks in her trial had been inspired by Till's death. Rosa Parks, herself, said she thought of Emmet Till when she was ordered to move seat and so was not prepared to move.

What are the strengths and weaknesses of Answer B?

This is a very good answer. It identifies two effects and clearly provides detailed support for both of them.

Challenge a friend

Use the Student Book to set a part (b) question for a friend. Then look at the answer. Does it do the following things?

☐ Provide two effects
☐ Provide 3–4 lines of detailed historical knowledge to explain why the event caused the outcomes (effects) they have identified.

If it does, you can tell your friend that the answer is very good!

3. THE IMPACT OF CIVIL RIGHTS PROTESTS, 1960–74

LEARNING OBJECTIVES

☐ Understand the civil rights protests of 1960–65

☐ Understand the impact of protest on the civil rights legislation of the 1960s

☐ Understand the reasons for the growth of black militancy and the impact of Black Power.

From 1960, the civil rights movement really grew, with an increased number and type of protests including sit-ins, freedom rides and marches. The vast majority of these protests were non-violent but they were often met with violence from white southerners. This brought further publicity to the civil rights movement and put pressure on the federal government to act. Eventually it did, with two pieces of landmark legislation: the 1964 Civil Rights Act and the 1965 Voting Rights Act.

The civil rights legislation, while important, did not bring equality for most African Americans. Many still lived in city ghettos with high levels of poverty. The continuing inequality caused riots in many cities across the USA. It was also a major reason for the rise of Black Nationalism, which took a more radical approach to try to improve the lives of African Americans.

3.1 PROTESTS, 1960–63

LEARNING OBJECTIVES

- Understand the sit-ins and their significance
- Understand the freedom rides and the response to them
- Understand the significance of the James Meredith case.

SIT-INS

The first major civil rights protests of the 1960s were not organised by well-known organisations such as the NAACP. Instead it was the actions of college students that began a new phase and style of non-violent direct action protest.

On 1 February 1960, four African American students from the North Carolina Agriculture and Technology College sat at the whites-only lunch counter in Woolworth's department store in Greensboro and waited to be served. They were asked to leave. Instead, the students remained, sitting patiently where they were until the shop closed. The next day, the same four students returned to Woolworth's and sat at the lunch counter. They were joined by another 25 students and they took turns to sit at the counter. On 3 February, 80 more students joined them. On 4 February, there were over 300 students. More students began **sit-ins** to try and desegregate lunch counters across Greensboro. Then they spread to other towns in North Carolina and finally to other towns across the whole of the South. Over 70,000 people took part in the sit-ins, which even spread to some northern states, like Ohio.

KEY TERM

sit-ins a type of protest in which people refuse to leave a place until their demands are considered or agreed to

THE RESPONSE TO THE SIT-INS

Those taking part in the sit-ins faced much abuse from some white segregationists. They were insulted and spat at, and regularly had food and drink thrown at them. Sometimes, they were even physically attacked. Despite sometimes extreme provocation, the protestors did not respond with violence. Thousands were arrested, which led to a new tactic of '**jail not bail**', so some jails became very overcrowded. These tactics attracted widespread media attention, which helped the sit-ins to spread: more people were inspired to take part in them – and support grew for their causes.

CIVIL RIGHTS GROUPS AND THE SIT-INS

The sit-ins seem to have taken existing civil rights organisations by surprise, but they were eager to support the protests once they knew the impact they were having. Activists from the NAACP, Congress of Racial Equality (CORE) and Southern Christian Leadership Council (SCLC) organised a boycott of shops with segregated lunch counters, at the same time as the sit-ins. CORE, which was mostly a Northern organisation with a significant number of white members, and the SCLC also helped to train students so they could become more effective protestors. This helped ensure that the students were always visible (for their safety and so that others, including the media, could see what was happening). It also prepared them to cope with the aggressive harassment they would face, so they would never respond with violence.

SUMMARY: CIVIL RIGHTS GROUPS

NAACP: National Association for the Advancement of Colored People

CORE: Congress of Racial Equality

SCLC: Southern Christian Leadership Council

MIA: Montgomery Improvement Association

SNCC: Student Nonviolent Co-ordinating Committee

ACMHR: Alabama Christian Movement for Human Rights

SOURCE A

Photo of Woolworth's lunch counter in Greensboro at the height of the sit-ins. Here 63 African Americans are waiting to be served, leaving just three empty seats for white customers.

Ella Baker, who had worked for both the NAACP and the SCLC, arranged for Martin Luther King to visit Greensboro and speak to the protestors to help maintain confidence. She also set up a meeting of students at Shaw University in Raleigh, North Carolina on 15 April 1960. King wanted the students to join the SCLC but Baker wanted them to set up their own civil rights group. At the meeting, the Student Nonviolent Co-ordinating Committee (the SNCC, known as 'snick') was set up and given a grant from the SCLC to help establish itself.

THE SIGNIFICANCE OF THE SIT-INS

The sit-ins proved to be very successful. The businesses affected by them suffered two-fold: they sold far fewer lunches as there were fewer seats available for white customers and they sold fewer goods in the stores because of the boycott. Most, including Woolworths, desegregated their eating facilities after sit-ins or the threat of them. Estimates vary but, by the end of 1960, over 120 towns and cities in the South had some desegregated lunch counters due to sit-ins. However, their success was not the only reason why the sit-ins were significant.

Sit-ins were more visible than boycotts, so everything could be seen by the public and the media. They generated huge publicity and the sight of young African Americans being attacked without retaliating attracted sympathy for their cause. Even President Eisenhower showed his concern: on 16 March 1960, he said he was 'deeply sympathetic with the efforts of any group to enjoy the rights of equality that they are guaranteed by the Constitution'.

The sit-ins were the first truly mass protest as huge numbers of people took part in them across a vast area. They were also the first protest that saw a significant number of white people protesting along with African Americans. Although older people did join the sit-ins and connected boycotts, most of the protesters were students. The sit-ins were the start of many student protests of the 1960s (see Chapter 4) and also saw the beginning of a new civil rights organisation specifically aimed at students – the SNCC.

Finally, the sit-ins were significant because they indicated a slight change of direction in the tactics of civil rights protestors. Although sit-ins were still a form of non-violent direct action, which had a big impact on the businesses targeted, they were more confrontational than previous protests. They could also be applied across a wide range of different facilities, such as beaches, hotels and libraries.

▶ **Figure 3.1** Significance of the sit-ins

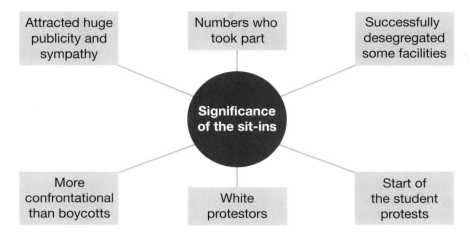

SOURCE B

From a book on the struggle for civil rights, published in 2010.

Soon there were wade-ins on the beaches, pray-ins in churches, read-ins in libraries… Whereas African Americans in Montgomery had protested segregation by staying away, this was protest by confrontation. By August 1961, over seventy thousand people had participated in some kind of direct-action protest. Hundreds of thousands more joined economic boycotts supporting the sit-ins. Within a year, over one hundred communities had desegregated their lunch counters some – starting with San Antonio, Texas, in March – to prevent sit-ins from even starting. On July 25, 1960, after renewed demonstrations, the lunch counter in Greensboro's Woolworth's served its first black customer.

ACTIVITY

1 Look at pages 29–33 on the Montgomery Bus Boycott. List ways in which sit-ins were a) similar and b) different to the Bus Boycott.
2 Write a paragraph explaining why sit-ins were a successful method of protest.

FREEDOM RIDERS

In December 1960, 4 years after its decision to desegregate state transport, the Supreme Court confirmed a ruling from 1946 that interstate transport should be desegregated. It also ordered that transport facilities, such as waiting rooms, had to be desegregated. In 1961, CORE activists planned 'freedom rides' to show that these rulings were not always being followed. CORE aimed to provoke a violent reaction that would generate huge publicity and force the Federal government to act (see Source C).

SOURCE C

James Farmer, founder of CORE, commenting on the aims of the freedom riders.

We planned the Freedom Rides with the specific intention of creating a crisis. We were counting on the bigots [intolerant people] in the South to do our work for us. We figured that the government would have to respond if we created a situation that was headline news all over the world, and affecting the nation's image abroad. An international crisis that was our strategy.

The first freedom riders left Washington DC on 4 May 1961 on two buses heading for the South. To begin with, there were few problems, but that all changed when the first bus reached Anniston, Alabama.

ANNISTON FIRE BOMBING

On 14 May, the first bus arrived at the station in Anniston, but the station, warned of potential trouble, had closed. The freedom riders were met by an angry crowd, led by local Ku Klux Klan leader William Chappell. The crowd attacked the bus; the windows and sides were smashed and the tyres damaged. The police arrived and cleared a path for the bus to leave. No one was arrested for the damage. A **police escort** led the bus to the outskirts of the city but then left, leaving the bus to the mob that had followed it. The damaged tyres finally burst, forcing the bus driver to pull over.

The mob tried to enter the bus and also tried to roll it over. Then, someone threw a firebomb through one of the broken windows into the bus. Others held the door shut while the bus was filled with smoke and the fire spread. As fire moved towards the petrol tank, the white mob left the bus, fearing an explosion. This allowed the passengers to escape, though some were attacked as they left the bus. **Highway** patrolmen prevented more attacks and the riders were taken by car to Birmingham airport.

The second bus was also attacked when it arrived in Anniston. The passengers were dragged off the bus and beaten up, but they were determined to complete their journey. They got back on the bus and continued to Montgomery, where they were again met by Klansmen and beaten. The police chief, 'Bull' Connor, ordered the police to do nothing.

SOURCE D

A cartoon called 'Anti-Freedom Rider', published in the *Washington Post*, 16 June 1961.

ACTIVITY

Study Source D. What is the message of this cartoon? (Hint: the runner on the right has the flag of the USA on his chest; the runner on the left has the flag of the Soviet Union on his chest.)

Anti-Freedom Rider

HERBLOCK
©1961 THE WASHINGTON POST CO.

THE FREEDOM RIDES CONTINUE

CORE arranged more freedom rides and the SNCC became involved as well. On 20 May, members of the press as well as freedom riders were attacked by hundreds of Klan members in Montgomery. This developed into attacks on the wider black community, but it was the freedom riders who were arrested for 'starting a riot'.

More and more people offered to be freedom riders, even though the violence and arrests continued. By the end of summer 1961, there had been over 60 freedom rides. Over 300 riders were sent to jail in Jackson, Mississippi, alone. Many more were beaten up.

But the freedom riders had achieved their aim – the continuing violence against them attracted huge media attention. The Federal government, under President Kennedy, was embarrassed by what the world was seeing. It threatened to send in US marshals to enforce desegregation of interstate buses and bus station facilities if states did not obey. The threat was enough and the states began to integrate bus facilities. This brought an end to the freedom rides by the end of 1961.

EXTRACT A

From a book on the history of civil rights, published in 2008.

What the lunch counter protests and the freedom rides achieved was to add a new dimension to civil rights protests. Although supporting non-violence, the students of SNCC and CORE forced Southern whites into violent retaliation by their actions. They had actively encouraged violent white resistance to highlight their case to American and world public opinion. In doing so, they forced President Kennedy to act.

ACTIVITY

1 List ways in which the freedom rides and sit-ins were similar and different.
2 Look at the diagram on page 45. Create a similar diagram on the significance of the freedom rides.

THE MEREDITH CASE

As with schools, the desegregation of universities occurred with varying degrees of success. Some integrated with little trouble. This was not the case with Mississippi University (known as 'Ole Miss'). When African American James Meredith applied for a place in May 1961, he was rejected. He went to the NAACP, which helped him to take his case to court. In June 1962, the Supreme Court ordered the university to admit him, but it still refused. The Governor of Mississippi had already said, on record, that 'no school will be integrated in Mississippi while I am your governor'. In September, with the governor's encouragement, the Mississippi state legislature quickly passed a law that denied admission to any person who had been convicted of any 'felony offense'. Meredith had previously been accused and convicted of 'false voter registration', so he was automatically suspended.

At this point, President Kennedy intervened. On 29 September, he ordered those 'obstructing the law' to 'desist'. On the same evening, there were riots on the university campus as white people who were opposed to Meredith joining the university protested. Kennedy sent hundreds of Federal officials, including marshals, to escort Meredith to register on 30 September. The officials were attacked and a riot followed. Kennedy's requests for calm were ignored, as two civilians died and 300 people (civilians and Federal marshals) were injured. Over 2,000 Federal troops were sent in by the president and they managed to stop the rioting.

On Monday 1 October, James Meredith successfully registered with Mississippi University. He was guarded by 300 state troops for the next year until he graduated.

EXTEND YOUR KNOWLEDGE

JAMES MEREDITH

Meredith took just 1 year to complete his degree in political science. During that year, he received constant verbal harassment from some white students and was avoided by others. That was not the end of his political activism, however. In 1966, he organised a March against Fear (see page 61) and was shot and injured during the march. He then became an active member of the Republican Party, and ran unsuccessfully for a seat in the House of Representatives in 1967 and then the Senate in 1972.

SOURCE E

Federal troops arriving in Mississippi on 30 September 1962 to stop the rioting that had erupted after James Meredith tried to enrol at the university.

ACTIVITY

Study Source E. Are you surprised by what it shows? Explain why you think this.

SIGNIFICANCE OF THE MEREDITH CASE

The Meredith case forced President Kennedy to act. This showed that the president would take direct action to enforce Supreme Court rulings if he had to. After this, African American students were rarely prevented from attending integrated universities by state or university authorities, although they often had a difficult time.

EXAM-STYLE QUESTION

A01   A02

Explain **two** effects of the freedom rides on the USA.   **(8 marks)**

HINT

You need to give only two effects when answering this question. You won't get credit for any more! You will get credit for adding details to explain the effects.

3.2 PROTESTS, 1963–65

LEARNING OBJECTIVES

- Understand the methods and activities of Martin Luther King
- Understand the impact of mass peace marches in Birmingham and Washington
- Understand the reasons for the failure of the Mississippi Freedom Summer and the events in Selma.

THE METHODS AND ACTIVITIES OF MARTIN LUTHER KING

Martin Luther King is probably the most famous civil rights campaigner. He was born in 1929 into a middle-class family. His father was a minister and Martin followed in his father's footsteps. He studied at Boston University, where he gained a doctorate. It was his work during the Montgomery Bus Boycott that made him well-known. After the 1963 March on Washington and his 'Dream' speech (see pages 51–53), King was seen as the leader of the civil rights movement.

King had many qualities that helped him to gain widespread support from people of all races, classes and ages.

- He was well educated, and a well-spoken and passionate speaker.
- He continually emphasised non-violence.
- He worked with people of all races.

Above all, King was a Baptist minister who therefore had the respect of many African Americans as many were committed Christians and most regularly attended church. Moreover, many Americans of all races had a strong Christian faith and were attracted to King's civil rights message that constantly emphasised Christian values and teachings from the Bible.

NON-VIOLENT DIRECT ACTION

King was heavily influenced and inspired by Mahatma Gandhi's non-violent protests, which had led to independence for India. Non-violence, no matter what the provocation, was at the heart of his beliefs. However, that did not mean that his methods were passive. He believed in direct action, such as boycotts and marches, which were often confrontational and dangerous for the protestors taking part. In fact, he realised that publicity was essential in bringing about change and therefore planned protests that he knew would cause a violent response from segregationists. He lived in constant fear of being attacked, and was arrested and imprisoned many times.

King's most important contribution to the civil rights movement was his speeches. He used these to win the support of many white people, including politicians, and to convince many African Americans and others to join the protests. He continually showed respect for the US system of government and the Constitution, which also won him supporters.

After 1965 King turned his attention to trying to tackle discrimination in the North, beginning in Chicago in 1966 (see page 66). His views began to change and he became increasingly disappointed and frustrated that the methods he had used to win legal reforms – protest and negotiation – failed to make much progress in ending discrimination or improving the lives of African Americans. His political views became more socialist, which lost him some supporters and led his campaigns to focus more on tackling poverty, unemployment and housing shortages for all Americans no matter what their race. Success was looking very unlikely when, on 4 April 1968, while visiting Memphis, Tennessee, to support a worker's strike he was assassinated. He never gave up his commitment to non-violence.

Martin Luther King's importance to civil rights is illustrated by the many roads, schools and institutions named after him today. The third Monday in January every year is Martin Luther King Day – a public holiday in the USA. There's little doubt that King did much for civil rights. However, people can exaggerate his importance and forget about the many other people who were involved in civil rights protests throughout the 1950s, 1960s and beyond.

EXTEND YOUR KNOWLEDGE

MAHATMA GANDHI

Mohandas Gandhi was an Indian who campaigned against racial segregation in South Africa while working there. He then led the movement for India to become free from British rule. He used the tactic of non-violent disobedience that inspired many others around the world, including Martin Luther King. Gandhi was widely referred to as 'Mahatma', meaning 'great soul'.

EXTRACT B

From a book on civil rights in the USA, published in 2008.

Clearly, Dr King had a large impact on how the civil rights movement was perceived by other Americans and by people around the world. His ability to speak eloquently [clearly and persuasively] and thoughtfully gave him a high profile in the age of television… However, it was not just the delivery of his speeches that made King so significant, it was also the message. His support for non-violent, peaceful protest elevated the civil rights cause to a high spiritual and religious level. As a… minister, he turned the civil rights cause into a religious movement… Through the use of the media and by linking the civil rights cause directly with the Declaration of Independence and the Constitution, King occupied the high moral and political ground.

EXAM-STYLE QUESTION

A04

SKILLS ANALYSIS, INTERPRETATION, CREATIVITY

Study Extract B.
What impression does the author give about the influence of Martin Luther King on the USA?
You **must** use Extract B to explain your answer. **(6 marks)**

HINT

Always read the extract several times and note down your thoughts in relation to the question before you begin your answer.

THE BIRMINGHAM PEACE MARCHES

The year of 1963 saw a huge explosion in civil rights protests across the USA. The first of these to achieve significant publicity was in Birmingham, Alabama. The Project C (for 'confrontation') campaign was led by the SNCC, SCLC and the Alabama Christian Movement for Human Rights (ACMHR). The campaigners aimed to end the rigid system of segregation in Birmingham, by co-ordinating sit-ins, boycotts and marches.

Part of the reason why Birmingham was chosen was because it had not desegregated any facilities at all. It also had an influential civil rights group (the ACMHR), which was well led by Reverend Fred Shuttlesworth. Nearly 45 per cent of the city's half a million inhabitants were African American, so there was the potential for very large numbers of protestors. Most of all, civil rights leaders knew that a campaign in Birmingham was likely to bring the publicity needed to force change. Birmingham had a very active Ku Klux Klan and African Americans were frequently attacked; African American homes and businesses had been bombed so often that the city was nicknamed 'Bombingham'. It was also where 'Bull' Connor (see page 46) was the police chief. Violence against the peaceful protesters seemed almost certain.

THE PROTESTS START

Thousands of people took part in Project C. The first **march** was on 3 April 1963 and was followed by other **demonstrations**. The police started arresting protestors. After a few weeks, most of the people who had taken part in marches were in jail, including Martin Luther King and Fred Shuttlesworth. The SNCC began training younger people in non-violent protest. On 2 May, the first large children's march took place. Although most of the marchers were teenagers, some were as young as 6 years old. Some people were shocked that children were being used as protestors; they became even more shocked by how they were treated. By the end of the day, around 1,000 children had been arrested. On 3 May, more children marched. This time, partly because the Birmingham jails were full, the police changed tactics. Chief Connor ordered dogs to be set on the protestors. He then called in the fire department to use powerful hoses on them. Connor's actions meant that the civil rights groups got the publicity they wanted: television **footage** and photographs of young people being attacked by dogs and fire hoses were shown throughout the world.

THE IMPACT OF BIRMINGHAM

President Kennedy sent a **negotiator** to Birmingham to help work out an agreement, and the mayor and protest leaders began talks on 10 May. However, state troops were sent in by the Governor of Alabama to disrupt the talks. This stirred up violence – including more bombings of African American homes and businesses. While protesting, African Americans did not respond with violence. However, the extreme violence against them on 11 and 12 May led to the first serious black riots. President Kennedy called in Federal troops to restore calm.

Most of the white business community preferred to make some **concessions** rather than continue to lose money through lost trade, so the mayor agreed to some desegregation. Most shops and lunch counters in Birmingham were desegregated, and African Americans were allowed to apply for some jobs that had previously been open to whites only. However, many facilities in Birmingham remained segregated and violence against African Americans continued.

KEY TERMS

march when a large group of people walk together to express their ideas or protest about something

demonstration an event at which a large group of people meet to protest or to support something in public

SOURCE F

From a television speech by President Kennedy on 11 June 1963.

We preach freedom around the world, and we mean it... But are we to say to the world – and much more importantly to one another – that this is the land of the free except for the Negroes? We face a moral crisis as a country and a people. It cannot be met by repressive police action. It cannot be left to increased demonstrations in our streets. It is a time to act in Congress and in our daily lives.

SOURCE G

Photographs like this one of attacks on peaceful demonstrators in Alabama in May 1963 shocked the world. President Kennedy said he felt 'sick and ashamed'.

Events in Birmingham led to similar protests across the USA and more cities began to desegregate facilities. Of greater significance was the impact that Birmingham had on the Federal government. The president wanted to avoid similar scenes in the future and he feared more general rioting might break out if nothing was done. His administration had begun working on a civil rights bill earlier in the year, but events in Birmingham gave it more importance.

THE MARCH ON WASHINGTON

Civil rights groups had wanted to organise a march on Washington for some time and detailed planning began soon after the Birmingham march. As the US capital city, Washington DC was the place where Federal government was based. The protestors wanted to show their support for the new civil rights bill that was being **debated**. They hoped that, if large numbers marched in support of the bill, the march would force the president and Congress to pass the bill. The organisers were not disappointed – the March on Washington would turn out to be the largest political gathering the USA had ever seen.

As news of the planned march spread, the Washington authorities were very worried about violence and rioting. President Kennedy tried to persuade the organisers to call it off, but they refused. To keep order, 1,000 extra police were brought in and 2,000 members of the National Guard were placed on stand-by. They were not needed. On 28 August 1963, exactly 100 years after **slavery** had ended, over 250,000 people, both African American and white, took part in the march for 'Jobs and Freedom'. They marched peacefully through the city to the Lincoln Memorial, where the National Anthem was sung followed by prayers, musical performances and speeches. The events were broadcast to the world live on television.

KEY TERM

slavery the system of having slaves

SOURCE H

Thousands took part in the March on Washington.

ACTIVITY

1 List the demands you can see in Source H made by those who marched on Washington.
2 Read the extract from the 'Dream' speech in Source I. If you can, find audio or video of the speech on the internet and listen to how King delivers it.
3 Discuss reasons why the speech has become so famous.

THE 'DREAM' SPEECH

Members from all the groups that had organised the march, including CORE, the NAACP, SNCC and SCLC, delivered speeches to the huge crowd. Martin Luther King was the final speaker. He had agreed to go last because nobody else had wanted to, believing that most of the crowd would have gone home by then. They did not. King used his great skill to deliver a speech that became one of the most famous in history. The speech made references to the US Constitution, the Declaration of Independence, Abraham Lincoln (the president who ended slavery), the Bible, hymns and sermons, and the idea of the '**American Dream**'. It emphasised Martin Luther King as the main leader of the civil rights movement. In 1964 he was awarded the Nobel Peace Prize.

KEY TERM

American Dream the idea that anyone in the USA can become wealthy and successful through hard work because everyone has the same opportunities and freedoms

THE 'DREAM' NEARLY DIDN'T HAPPEN!

Martin Luther King had often spoken about his 'dream' in previous speeches and was advised not to use it again. Therefore, King and his advisers didn't include any references to a dream when they wrote the speech the night before the March on Washington. However, a few minutes into his speech, King decided to go off-script after Mahalia Jackson, a gospel singer who was a friend of his, shouted out: 'Tell 'em about the dream, Martin'. He pushed his notes to one side and instead of the speech he had planned, he told the world about his dream.

KENNEDY'S ASSASSINATION

On 22 November 1963, Kennedy was travelling through Dallas, Texas, in an open convertible car, with his wife, the Governor of Texas and the governor's wife. During the journey, Kennedy was shot three times by Lee Harvey Oswald. Two days later, as he was being taken to jail, Oswald was shot and killed by Jack Ruby. Investigations concluded that Oswald and Ruby had both acted alone, but there have been many conspiracy theories about who was behind Kennedy's assassination. The most popular suspects include: the CIA, the KGB, Cuban exiles, Vice President Johnson and even Kennedy's wife!

THE FAILURE OF THE MISSISSIPPI FREEDOM SUMMER

KEY TERM

assassinate murder an important person

SOURCE I

From Martin Luther King's 'Dream' speech, delivered at the Lincoln Memorial, Washington, 28 August 1963.

… I still have a dream. It is a dream deeply rooted in the American Dream. I have a dream that one day this nation will rise up and live out the true meaning of its creed: 'We hold these truths to be self-evident, that all men are created equal.'

I have a dream that one day on the red hills of Georgia sons of former slaves and the sons of former slave-owners will be able to sit down together at the table of brotherhood. I have a dream that one day even the state of Mississippi, a state sweltering with the heat of injustice, sweltering with the heat of oppression, will be transformed into an oasis of freedom and justice.

I have a dream that my four little children will one day live in a nation where they will not be judged by the color of their skin but by the content of their character.

THE IMPORTANCE OF THE MARCH ON WASHINGTON

There were several reasons why the March on Washington was a very important event in the civil rights movement.

- The huge number of people who took part showed that civil rights was supported by many people, African American and white. Many observers were impressed by the organisation of such a large protest and the fact that it was peaceful.
- The event brought huge publicity to the cause, due to the size of the protest and the presence of many celebrities, such as singer-songwriter Bob Dylan, and actors Paul Newman and Marlon Brando.
- It put further pressure on politicians, as it took place during the period when a civil rights bill was being debated in Congress.
- It really fixed Martin Luther King's place as leader of the whole civil rights movement.

After the march ended on 28 August 1963, civil rights leaders met President Kennedy and Vice President Johnson in the White House. The President assured the protestors that the Federal government was committed to seeing the civil rights bill through Congress. Everyone knew this would not be an easy task. To many civil rights supporters, it seemed even more unlikely when President Kennedy was **assassinated** in November 1963. Vice President Johnson, a Democrat from the Southern state of Texas, became the new president.

Since 1961, civil rights groups had campaigned to improve the number of African Americans who were registered to vote throughout the South and had met with some success. They were supported by the president's brother, Bobby Kennedy. A presidential election was due in November 1964, so the NAACP, CORE and SNCC stepped up the campaign with 'Freedom Summer' during the summer months of that year. This campaign focused on Mississippi, which had the lowest percentage of African Americans registered to vote in any state: fewer than 7 per cent. In order to register to vote in Mississippi, African Americans had to pass an extremely difficult literacy test. The few who passed the test were then often beaten or threatened with violence to prevent them from registering.

The Freedom Summer campaign involved setting up a new political party – the Mississippi Freedom Democratic Party (the MFDP). This party had more than 80,000 members, and 68 members were elected to join the national Democratic Party convention in that year. This was a direct challenge to Mississippi's all-white Democratic Party. The MFDP ran classes to help African Americans pass voter registration tests. It also opened 30 Freedom Schools throughout Mississippi, which taught black history and politics.

The SNCC recruited around 1,000 volunteers to travel to Mississippi and help in the Freedom Summer projects. Most volunteers were young, white college students from well-off Northern families. They were chosen because they could afford to support themselves but also because the SNCC knew that any violence against young, white people would generate big headlines.

THE FREEDOM SUMMER MURDERS

Unsurprisingly, those who took part in the Freedom Summer were attacked by the Ku Klux Klan, which had a very large membership in Mississippi. Freedom campaigners were shot or beaten up, and African American churches and homes were bombed. On 21 June 1964, three campaigners – Michael Scherner, Andrew Goodman and James Chaney (who were members of CORE) – were arrested for traffic offences when driving to Scherner's house in Mississippi. The policeman who arrested them was a Klan member and told others that he had the three men in custody. After they were released from prison, they were never seen again. Six weeks later, their bodies were discovered. Scherner and Goodman had been shot in the chest, Chaney had been beaten to death.

Their deaths attracted huge publicity and support for civil rights, but they also caused some divisions within civil rights groups: some black members suspected that the publicity was so huge because Scherner and Goodman were white. Some African American activists began to look for more radical solutions.

Many people see the Freedom Summer campaign as a failure. Its aims were to increase voter registration, but only 1,600 more African Americans successfully registered to vote in Mississippi (although over 17,000 tried to do so). Most failed to register even though the teaching they had received enabled them to pass the literacy tests. Many of the African Americans were frightened into not registering by being threatened with violence. Some were physically attacked or had their property attacked. Others were threatened with dismissal from work if they registered to vote. However, there were some successes with the setting up of the MFDP and the 30 Freedom Schools, which improved African American literacy rates. Moreover, the publicity generated by the murders did increase support for civil rights and brought the problems of voter registration to national attention.

ACTIVITY

1 Give reasons why the Freedom Summer failed to register many more African American voters.
2 Create a table of reasons why the Freedom Summer was a failure and why it was a success.

SELMA AND VOTING RIGHTS

Dallas County in Alabama had an even worse percentage of registered black voters than Mississippi. Selma was the main city in the county and, in January 1965, local civil rights groups invited Martin Luther King and the SCLC to campaign there. For 2 months, there were protests and attempts to register African Americans to vote. This led to violent confrontations with the police and many arrests, and one protester was murdered. The lack of success led the SCLC to change tactics.

SOURCE J

A protest march held in New York on 15 March 1965 as a result of the events in Selma on 7 March.

On Sunday 7 March, a protest march left Selma, heading to the state capital, Montgomery. Just outside Selma, at the Edmund Pettus Bridge, the march was stopped by police. State troops and police attacked the protestors with tear gas, horses, clubs and electric cattle sticks. It became known as 'Bloody Sunday' and, yet again, footage of African Americans being attacked was broadcast around the world.

A second march was organised 2 days later, but Martin Luther King would not let marchers confront state police, so the march was called off. However, the president used the events of the first march at Selma to persuade members of Congress to support a voting rights bill. Meanwhile, protestors from all over the USA set off for Selma, determined to show their support.

On 17 March, Johnson submitted a voting rights bill to Congress. He then took control of the Alabama National Guard and the march from Selma to Montgomery finally took place from 21 March, escorted by these troops. On 25 March, Martin Luther King led around 25,000 people to the state **capitol** in Montgomery. In August, Congress passed the Voting Rights Act (see page 56).

There was another major impact of Selma, however, as some historians believe this is where the civil rights movement began to split. Many of the protestors, including SNCC members, wanted to directly confront the police and more began to question non-violence as a strategy. It would lead to more militant protests (see Section 3.4) in the years ahead.

KEY TERM

capitol a building where a legislature/ parliament meets

3.3 CIVIL RIGHTS LEGISLATION

LEARNING OBJECTIVES

- Understand the Civil Rights Act of 1964
- Understand the Voting Rights Act of 1965
- Understand the reasons for these pieces of legislation, including the impact of protests.

THE CIVIL RIGHTS ACT, 1964

The Civil Rights bill was struggling in Congress when President Kennedy was assassinated in November 1963. His successor, Lyndon Johnson, used the shock and horror of Kennedy's death – along with every other method he could think of – to persuade and bully members of Congress to support the bill without amendments. It was still a close thing, as Dixiecrats managed a 54-day filibuster attempt, but Johnson had enough support from both Democrats and Republicans. On 2 July 1964, he signed the Civil Rights Act.

▶ Figure 3.2 Terms of the 1964 Civil Rights Act

Civil Rights Act, 1964

- Segregation and discrimination in public places, education and businesses banned.
- Voter registration tests had to be fair and the same for black and white people.
- Discrimination in employment banned and the Equal Opportunities Commission established to investigate discrimination in employment.
- The federal government could remove funding from state projects that discriminated.

EXTEND YOUR KNOWLEDGE

NOT JUST FOR AFRICAN AMERICANS
The 1964 Civil Rights Act made it illegal to discriminate on the basis of gender, religion or national origin, as well as race. Some people believe that Howard Smith, a Democrat from Virginia, introduced the word 'sex' to the bill because he believed that this would persuade others not to pass it. However, Smith himself maintained that he genuinely wanted to help women. (See Section 4.3 for more on the Women's movement.)

The passing of the Civil Rights Act was very significant and a huge achievement, as it ended legal segregation. However, the act did not mean the end of discrimination, as it was very difficult to enforce the laws, especially in the Deep South. Many Southerners were angered by the extent of the act while many African Americans felt that it did not go far enough.

THE VOTING RIGHTS ACT, 1965

The original civil rights bill had contained more to try and increase the number of African American voters but Johnson removed these sections, fearing that the bill would never be passed if they remained. However, the events of the Freedom Summer and Selma highlighted the many issues that prevented African Americans from voting and the need for the law to help with this. During the events in Selma (see pages 54–55), Johnson began trying to persuade members of Congress to support a voting rights bill. He managed to get this bill through Congress in record time. It became law on 6 August 1965.

▶ **Figure 3.3** Terms of the Voting Rights Act

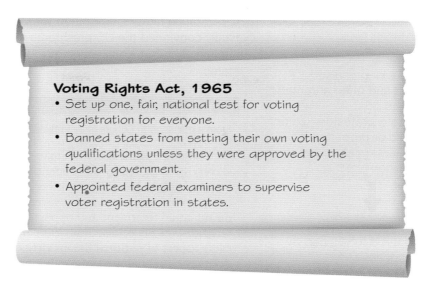

Voting Rights Act, 1965
- Set up one, fair, national test for voting registration for everyone.
- Banned states from setting their own voting qualifications unless they were approved by the federal government.
- Appointed federal examiners to supervise voter registration in states.

After the Voting Rights Act, there was a dramatic increase in the number of African Americans registered to vote in some Southern states (see Source K).

SOURCE K

Percentage of eligible African Americans registered to vote.

	ALABAMA	GEORGIA	LOUISIANA	MISSISSIPPI
1964	19.3	27.4	31.6	6.7
1968	61.3	60.4	60.8	67.5

Many historians believe that the Voting Rights Act was even more important than the Civil Rights Act of 1964. It meant that African Americans began to gradually elect representatives from their own communities at local, city and then national level. It also meant that, for the first time, issues which affected African Americans had to be considered by politicians who wanted to win their votes.

THE IMPACT OF PROTEST ON CIVIL RIGHTS LEGISLATION

In 1947, President Truman had stated that he wanted laws to improve civil rights for African Americans. However, it was nearly 20 years before the really significant legislation of 1964 and 1965 was passed. Many members of Congress did not believe there was a need for civil rights laws and many Southern senators (and those who had elected them), were strongly opposed to improving civil rights for African Americans. So what were the reasons for legislation being submitted and, more importantly, approved in the mid-1960s?

The protests of the civil rights movement were essential for several reasons, as shown in Figure 3.4. There were also a number of other factors, such as:
- the attitudes of presidents – both Kennedy and Johnson – and the political skill and hard work of President Johnson in getting legislation passed
- more people in Congress who wanted to 'do the right thing'
- the emergence of more radical activists (see Section 3.4), who seemed to threaten violent protest if legislation was not passed.

▼ **Figure 3.4** Impact of protests on civil rights legislation

Protests were:
- well led and well organised
- highly visible and often attracted large numbers
- within the law – protestors did not attack people or property
- targeted in areas likely to get an extreme reaction

As a result, this:
- highlighted the issues faced by African Americans
- showed the numbers in support of civil rights
- often provoked a violent reaction, showing their opponents did not operate within the law

The effect was:
- increased awareness and therefore further support for civil rights
- huge publicity both within the USA and internationally

All put pressure on the federal government to act.

It was these factors, combined with the impacts of the civil rights protests, that finally convinced the US presidents to introduce civil rights legislation, even if this meant that – as Democrats – they would lose the votes of the Southern states.

SOURCE L

From a message to Congress by President Kennedy on 28 February 1963.

One hundred years ago, the Emancipation Proclamation [the measure to end slavery] was signed by a President who believed in the equal worth of every human being… [But] While slavery has vanished, progress for the Negro has been too often blocked and delayed. Equality before the law has not always meant equal treatment and opportunity. And the harmful, wasteful and wrongful results of discrimination and segregation still appear in virtually every aspect of national life, in virtually every part of the Nation… Race discrimination hampers our economic growth by preventing the maximum development and utilization of our manpower. It hampers our world leadership by contradicting at home the message we preach abroad. It mars the atmosphere of a united and classless society in which this nation rose to greatness. It increases the costs of public welfare, crime, delinquency and disorder. Above all, it is wrong.

SOURCE M

From President Johnson's speech after signing the Voting Rights Act, 6 August 1965.

And then last March, with the outrage of Selma still fresh, I came down to this Capitol one evening and asked the Congress and the people for swift and for sweeping action to guarantee to every man and woman the right to vote. In less than 48 hours I sent the Voting Rights Act of 1965 to the Congress. In little more than 4 months the Congress, with overwhelming majorities, enacted one of the most monumental laws in the entire history of American freedom.

ACTIVITY

1 Read Source L. List the reasons for change given by President Kennedy.
2 Read Source M. What does President Johnson suggest was the impact of Selma?
3 Write a paragraph explaining how the civil rights protests put pressure on the government to pass civil rights legislation.

3.4 PROTESTS, 1966–74

LEARNING OBJECTIVES

- [ ] Understand the reasons for the growth of Black Power and its impact, including the influence of Malcolm X and Stokely Carmichael
- [ ] Understand the Black Panther movement and the roles of Bobby Seale and Huey Newton
- [ ] Understand the impact of race riots.

KEY TERM

Black Nationalism the desire by certain African Americans to form an independent country

From 1966, different kinds of civil rights protest began to emerge. This was because not all African Americans agreed with the methods of the civil rights movement, such as peaceful protest, integration and working with the government. Some groups argued for **Black Nationalism**, which meant living completely separately from other races. They felt that violence could be justified as a means of achieving equality.

THE NATION OF ISLAM AND MALCOLM X

One Black Nationalist group was the Nation of Islam. It had been set up in July 1930 and, along with some common Muslim beliefs, had always argued that racial integration would not bring equality or end discrimination because white people would always consider themselves superior. Instead, African Americans should be segregated from whites but should have the same standard of facilities, until they were able to have their own state. The Nation of Islam was a collection of very small groups and only had 500 members in 1952. Within 10 years, however, it had grown massively to over 40,000 members. Many people believe this was due to the influence of Malcolm X.

THE WORK OF MALCOLM X

Malcolm Little joined the Nation of Islam while he was in prison for burglary during the 1940s. He changed his name to 'X' because 'Little' was the name given to his ancestors by their slave owner. On leaving prison in 1952, he became a minister for the Nation of Islam before becoming its representative. He spoke with great passion and skill, and travelled all over the USA trying to convert people.

Malcolm X was very critical of the civil rights movement and leaders like Martin Luther King. He referred to the March on Washington as the 'Farce on Washington' and saw it as an attempt to please white people. He also thought that not retaliating to white violence was foolish. However, he went further than this and felt that violence could be justified as a means of achieving a separate black nation.

Many of the civil rights activists saw Malcolm X as extreme and dangerous, but he won supporters because he seemed to understand the social and financial problems faced by many African Americans that the civil rights movement had failed to address.

EXTEND YOUR KNOWLEDGE

MALCOLM X'S FAMILY

Malcolm X's parents were supporters of Black Nationalism and were often attacked by violent racist groups. His father, a Baptist minister, was hit by a tram and later died when Malcolm was six. The authorities ruled that it had been an accident, but many believed that he had been beaten and placed on the tracks by the Black Legion, a white supremacist group. Malcolm's uncle was lynched by another group of racists.

ACTIVITY

1 Read Source N. Explain what you think Malcolm X means by 'any means necessary'.
2 If possible, find some footage of Malcolm X's speeches on the internet. Discuss in groups what you think the reaction of white Americans would be to Malcolm X.

SOURCE N

An extract from a speech by Malcolm X at the Founding Rally of the Organization of Afro-American Unity, 29 June 1964.

So we have formed an organization known as the Organization of Afro-American Unity, which has the same aim and objective – to fight whoever gets in our way, to bring about the complete independence of people of African descent here in the Western Hemisphere, and first here in the United States, and bring about the freedom of these people by any means necessary.

That's our motto. We want freedom by any means necessary. We want justice by any means necessary. We want equality by any means necessary. We don't feel that in 1964, living in a country that is supposedly based upon freedom, and supposedly the leader of the free world, we don't think that we should have to sit around and wait for some segregationist congressmen and senators and a President from Texas in Washington DC, to make up their minds that our people are due now some degree of civil rights. No, we want it now or we don't think anybody should have it.

MALCOLM X'S LATER VIEWS AND LEGACY

In 1964, Malcolm X left the Nation of Islam after arguing with its leader, Elijah Muhamad, who was jealous of Malcolm's reputation and success. His religious views changed to become more similar to traditional Islam and he went on pilgrimage to Mecca, the most sacred place in Islam. While he was there, he saw Muslims of all races treating each other equally and he began to change his views on Black Nationalism. On returning to the United States, he set up the Organization of Afro-American Unity as a civil rights group that would also promote close links with people in Africa. He said the organisation would work with other civil rights groups, even those with many white members.

However, he never got the chance to do this. On 21 February 1965, while making a speech in New York, he was assassinated by three members of the Nation of Islam who were angry that he had left the group and changed his views.

Malcolm X's influence increased after his death. His ideas of black pride, violence in self-defence and a rejection of the civil rights movement inspired many others and became the basis of more radical groups, such as Black Power and the Black Panthers. However, he also had an impact on all civil rights groups by highlighting the huge economic and social problems facing many African Americans.

SOURCE O

Malcolm X speaking at a Nation of Islam rally in New York City in 1963.

BLACK POWER

Despite the changes in the law brought by the Civil Rights Act in 1964 and the Voting Rights Act in 1965, African Americans still faced discrimination and violence. In June 1966, James Meredith (see pages 47–48) led a 'March Against Fear' through Mississippi to highlight the violence still faced by African Americans. He was shot on the second day of the march. While he recovered, Martin Luther King and Stokely Carmichael took over leadership of the march. Their speeches struck very different tones. King continued to highlight the need for peaceful protest, but Carmichael's speeches were more militant. He encouraged people to demand 'Black Power'.

SOURCE P

From the speech made by Stokely Carmichael in June 1966, following his release from police custody during the 'March Against Fear'.

This is the 27th time I have been arrested. I ain't going to jail no more. The only way we gonna stop them white men from whuppin' [beating] us is to take over. We been saying 'freedom' for six years and we ain't got nothin'. What we gonna start sayin' now is 'Black Power'!

THE INFLUENCE OF STOKELY CARMICHAEL

Carmichael had been a well-known campaigner for the SNCC since the Freedom Rides and became the group's leader in May 1966. Although he had supported the policy of non-violent direct action, Carmichael was frustrated and annoyed by the slow progress this had brought. Many of his ideas were influenced by Malcom X – for example, rejecting white help, taking a more radical approach to improving the lives of African Americans, and celebrating African culture. Non-violence was no longer essential and people were encouraged to defend themselves if attacked. White people were no longer welcome as members of the SNCC. This marked a turning point in the civil rights movement, as the separate groups that made up the movement broke apart in their ideas and approach.

Carmichael was one of the first people to use the term 'Black Power' and it rapidly gained popularity. It was particularly attractive to young African Americans from poor communities who wanted a more radical method to improve their lives.

REASONS FOR THE GROWTH OF BLACK POWER

The Black Power movement grew both because of its own attractions and because of the problems with other civil rights groups.

- Many African Americans were frustrated by the slow progress made by the traditional approach of civil rights campaigns. Segregation and discrimination continued to damage black people's lives, and changes in the law had not helped.
- Black Power expressed the anger felt by many African Americans about the lack of employment opportunities and worsening conditions in city **ghettos**. Groups campaigned on local issues, which often got results (see Black Panthers on page 63).
- The change in the SNCC and the rise of Black Power groups, as well as events at the 1968 Olympics (see below), gained much publicity. This increased awareness and encouraged people to join the movement.
- Black Power groups encouraged African Americans to be proud of their race, culture and heritage, which was attractive to many people. They also encouraged African Americans to defend themselves if they were attacked.

ACTIVITY

What do you think when you think of the term 'Black Power'? Discuss different meanings of the term in groups.

KEY TERM

ghetto a part of a city where people of a particular race or class live separately

THE 1968 OLYMPICS

In 1968, the Olympics were held in Mexico. Some African Americans called for a boycott of the Olympics by black athletes, but most athletes wanted their chance to perform on a world stage. Some found another way of protesting. Tommie Smith and John Carlos won the gold and bronze medals in the 200 metre sprint. During the US national anthem at the medal ceremony, they gave the Black Power salute of a clenched fist. They also wore black socks without shoes to highlight the poverty of African Americans. As they left the stadium, they were shouted at by Americans in the crowd. They were criticised by many in the media and even received death threats. They were also banned from future Olympics. However, their protest inspired many young black Americans to join Black Power groups and, as it was seen by millions of people, it brought the Black Power movement worldwide attention.

SOURCE Q

Tommie Smith (centre) and John Carlos (right) giving the Black Power salute beside Peter Norman (left) in the medal ceremony for the 200 metre sprint at the 1968 Mexico Olympics.

EXTEND YOUR KNOWLEDGE

THE FORGOTTEN MAN

The man who won silver in the 200 metres at the 1968 Olympics was Australian Peter Norman (left in Source Q). It was he who suggested that Smith and Carlos should wear a glove each as Carlos had forgotten his pair of gloves. He also borrowed an 'Olympic Project for Human Rights' badge from a member of the US rowing team to wear during the ceremony, to show his support for the Black Power cause. Norman returned home in disgrace and was never picked for another Australian team. After that day, Peter Norman became friends with Smith and Carlos. They both helped to carry his coffin at his funeral in 2006.

THE IMPACT OF BLACK POWER

Black Power worried moderate African American civil rights supporters and it terrified many white Americans. Some people blamed Black Power for the race riots (see pages 64–65), while others held the movement responsible for the increase in police actions against all civil rights activists. However, the movement also had a positive impact on many African Americans. It continued the work of Malcolm X and led to more African Americans taking pride in their culture and heritage. This helped raise the self-confidence and belief of many young black people. It also inspired many projects which aimed to improve living conditions. Indeed, Black Power's focus on the economic and social problems of African Americans brought increased awareness of these issues and influenced the campaigns and focus of the civil rights movement after 1965.

THE BLACK PANTHERS

Huey Newton and Bobby Seale set up the Black Panther Party in October 1966 in Oakland, California. The Black Panthers were probably the best known Black Power group and also one of the most feared, although they never had more than about 2,000 members across groups in 25 cities. Members wore black berets, trousers and leather jackets, so they were highly visible. They often carried guns. Unlike most other Black Power groups, the party was willing to work with white people who shared its beliefs.

The aims of the Black Panthers were outlined in a ten-point plan (see Figure 3.5), but the media was most interested in the campaign that became known as 'patrolling the pigs'. In this campaign, Panthers would follow police officers to prevent abuse of African Americans. Many people in the ghettos saw the Panthers as a more effective police force than the actual police, though there were frequent shoot-outs and violence that attracted negative publicity. The Black Panthers were seen as a great threat by the government because of their socialist beliefs (see page 16). Members were heavily watched by the FBI.

▶ **Figure 3.5** The Black Panthers' ten-point plan

Ten-point Plan

1 We want freedom. We want the power to run our black community.

2 We want full employment for our people.

3 We want an end to the robbery by the white man of our black community.

4 We want decent housing fit for shelter of human beings.

5 We want education for our people that exposes the true nature of this decadent American society. We want education that teaches us our true history and our role in present-day society.

6 We want all black men to be free from having to serve in the military forces.

7 We want an immediate end to Police brutality and murder of black people.

8 We want freedom for all black men held in prisons, federal or state, because they have not received a fair trial.

9 We want all black people who are brought to trial to be tried by a jury from their black community.

10 We want land, bread, housing, education, clothing, justice and peace.

Kansas City Black Panther Bill Whitfield serves breakfast to local children as part of the Panther free breakfast program, 16 April 1969.

ACTIVITY

1 Read the Black Panthers' ten-point plan. In what ways were the aims of the Black Panthers a) similar and b) different to other groups, such as the SCLC?

2 'The Black Panthers had only a small number of members so they were never really a concern to the authorities.' Explain whether or not you agree with this statement.

Black Panther groups were particularly successful with some of their schemes to try and improve life in ghettos. They:
- organised medical clinics to give black people free healthcare
- ran breakfast clubs for black children to attend before school
- provided free shoes for poor black families
- ran classes on black history
- encouraged co-operation between different African American gangs to reduce violence.

Money for their projects was raised from donations, mostly given by black businesses. It was also sometimes gained through theft.

EXAM-STYLE QUESTION

A01   **A02**

SKILLS   PROBLEM SOLVING, REASONING, DECISION MAKING, ADAPTIVE LEARNING, INNOVATION

'The main impact of the Black Power movement was to drive away white supporters of civil rights for African Americans.'

How far do you agree? Explain your answer.

You may use the following in your answer:
- driving away white supporters of civil rights
- improving life in the ghettos.

You **must** also use information of your own.   **(16 marks)**

HINT

Don't forget to write about examples other than the two given in the bullet points.

RACE RIOTS

In July 1964, a large race riot took place in New York, just 2 weeks after the signing of the Civil Rights Act. This shows that there was still much unhappiness within African American communities, as people realised that laws alone would not bring about equality. Over the next 4 years, there were 329 major riots in 257 American cities. Over 200 people were killed, thousands were injured, tens of thousands were arrested, and property and goods worth billions of dollars were damaged.

The largest riot was in the Watts district of Los Angeles between 11 and 17 August 1965. Marquette Frye was arrested on suspicion of drink-driving by two police officers. He resisted arrest and rumours spread through the neighbourhood that the police had attacked his mother and pregnant girlfriend. Violent protests broke out. Over 14,000 California National Guard troops enforced a **curfew zone** of approximately 70 km to try and restore order. After 6 days, 34 people had died, over 1,000 were injured, nearly 4,000 were arrested and hundreds of shops, businesses and homes had been badly damaged.

None of the riots was organised by any group and most of the people who took part were young African Americans. City authorities blamed the influence of Black Power, but the 1968 Kerner Report – set up to investigate the riots – said the riots had been caused by:

- frustration and anger at the poor living conditions in the ghettos caused by segregation and discrimination
- failure of the police and city authorities to respond to reported problems
- unfair treatment, and sometimes violence, by the police whose use of extreme violence during the riots made the situation worse.

The Kerner Report recommended setting up more social programmes to deal with these problems. However, Richard Nixon became president in January 1969 and these recommendations were never followed up.

SOURCE S

From the introduction to the Kerner Report, 1968.

This is our basic conclusion: Our nation is moving toward two societies, one black, one white – separate and unequal. Reaction to last summer's disorders has quickened the movement and deepened the division. Discrimination and segregation have long been a part of much of American life; they now threaten the future of every American. This deepening racial division is not inevitable. The movement apart can be reversed. Choice is still possible.

EXTRACT C

From a book about the history and culture of the USA, published in 1996.

Despite the civil rights gains of the 1960s, however, racial discrimination and repression remained a significant factor in American life. Even after President Johnson declared a war on poverty and King initiated a Poor People's Campaign in 1968, the distribution of the nation's wealth and income moved towards greater inequality in the 1970s. Civil rights advocates acknowledged that desegregation had not brought significant improvement in the lives of poor blacks.

EXAM-STYLE QUESTION

A04

SKILLS   ANALYSIS, INTERPRETATION, CREATIVITY

Study Extract C.
What impression does the author of Extract C give about progress made in African American civil rights?

You **must** use Extract C to explain your answer.   **(6 marks)**

HINT

Remember that you only need to use the extract itself to answer this type of question. Writing about your own opinions will waste time and not gain any marks.

IMPACT OF THE RIOTS

The rioting lost the sympathy of some white supporters of civil rights and made some white people more afraid of young African Americans. This was partly due to the exaggerated reporting of the riots by the media. Money was given by the Federal government to improve conditions in the ghettos, but this was often spent on weapons and training for police so they could deal with the riots themselves rather than the problems that caused them.

There were some more positive impacts of the riots. They helped to change the focus of some civil rights campaigners on to the social and economic problems that many black Americans faced in their everyday lives. Rioting also widened the area of civil rights campaigns, before this point most campaigns had focused on the South. However, to many white Americans, rioting by African Americans seemed to signify the end of the largely non-violent civil rights campaigns up until this point.

THE MAINSTREAM CIVIL RIGHTS MOVEMENT, 1966–74

On 7 January 1966, the SCLC and its leader, Martin Luther King, announced that their campaigns in the North would begin in Chicago with the Chicago Freedom Movement. Areas of Chicago were ghettos where African Americans faced terrible living conditions. Most lived there because these were the only places where they could afford the rents.

The campaign focused on three main issues – improving housing, education and employment. 'Operation Breadbasket' held boycotts to try and pressure businesses into employing more black people, whilst King and other civil rights leaders met with city officials to try and reach agreements on improving housing conditions. Progress was very slow and King had great difficulty in persuading protestors not to retaliate to violence they faced. In July, race riots broke out. During a protest march in August, protestors were attacked with rocks, bricks and bottles. Later in August, King managed to reach an agreement with Chicago's mayor who was keen to end the protests, to build public housing and for the Mortgage Bankers Association to agree mortgages regardless of race. However, these agreements were not upheld by the Chicago authorities.

The Poor People's Campaign, announced in December 1967, was another campaign by King and the SLCL. It was designed to help poor people of all races. Mexican Americans, Native Americans and poor white Americans joined the campaign which wanted:
- an extension of welfare to help the unemployed
- a fair minimum wage
- education for poor adults as well as children to improve their self-esteem and their chances of getting a good job.

The campaign was focused on Washington DC, where thousands of people set up temporary shelters near the Congress building ready to protest. Despite King's assassination in April, the campaign went ahead in June 1968. However, without King to hold them together, the different groups disagreed on the tactics to be used in the protest and many supporters left Washington even before a planned march took place. The campaign did have some small successes, such as setting up free food programmes in poorer areas, but, in reality, its poor organisation meant it was generally seen as a disaster which damaged the public image of the civil rights movement.

BUSSING AND AFFIRMATIVE ACTION
President Johnson was worried by the increase in African American violence and the more extreme nature of the civil rights campaigns after 1965. He hoped that government action on civil rights might help reduce the level of extremism. The Civil Rights Act of 1964 confirmed the *Brown* ruling that Federal funding could be cut to those schools who resisted integration.

EXTEND YOUR KNOWLEDGE

THE IMPACT OF KING'S DEATH
Martin Luther King was shot outside a motel by a white supremacist on 4 April 1968. An explosion of riots broke out across America. The violence caused by his death did huge damage to the movement, as it seemed that King's message of non-violence had been totally forgotten. The civil rights movement was always made up of groups with slightly different opinions, but Martin Luther King had mostly managed to keep these groups together. That unity was lost once he was killed.

Johnson used this very effectively so that by the end of his presidency in 1968, 60 per cent of Southern schools had desegregated.

One method that schools used to desegregate was **bussing**. It was highly controversial. Many people objected because they did not want their children having to travel across town or objected to mixed-race education. In some towns white families moved out of urban areas because they did not want their children to be educated alongside black children.

President Nixon (1969–74) was less committed to civil rights than Johnson had been. Bussing continued during his presidency, but he was far less active in reducing funding in schools that did not comply with desegregation. The NAACP continued to challenge districts where schools refused or were slow to integrate by taking them to court. In 1971, it took the case of *Swann versus Charlotte-Mecklenburg Board of Education* to the Supreme Court. As part of the ruling, the Supreme Court decided that bussing was allowed. Nixon spoke out against bussing on television and tried, unsuccessfully, to overturn the ruling. However, in the case of *Milliken versus Bradley* in 1974, the Supreme Court ruled that bussing was allowed only where segregation was deliberate and was not allowed across different school districts. Therefore, schools in white areas that were a district away from black areas effectively did not have to integrate. Bussing had already started to decline and by the end of 1974, integration of Southern schools had dropped to 40 per cent.

Johnson also encouraged a policy of **affirmative action**, where schools or businesses allowed African Americans to study or get jobs even if, for example, they had lower qualifications than other candidates. This was extremely controversial and many black Americans objected to it as well as white Americans, who felt they were being unfairly treated. Nixon continued the policy of affirmative action. For example, in 1969, he approved the Philadelphia plan where building contractors were set targets to employ African Americans. This increased black workers from 1 to 12 per cent of the total work force. The policy of affirmative action was declared constitutional by the Supreme Court in the case of *Griggs versus Duke Power Company* in 1971.

Although Nixon pushed the Equal Opportunity Act of 1972 through Congress, generally he did little for civil rights. Many of his Republican supporters did not want to see further action on civil rights and he was also looking to win support from former Democrat supporters in the South.

Therefore, between 1968 and 1974 there were a few improvements in the areas of education and employment but little progress in other areas. This was because civil rights groups were divided and without an overall leader after Martin Luther King's death and there was no longer a president committed to pushing for further reform. Many African Americans continued to live in great poverty and achieving real equality still seemed a long way away – despite the great legal progress that had been made.

KEY TERMS

bussing where buses were used to transport children from mainly black areas to mainly white areas (or the opposite) to go to school

affirmative action positive discrimination to give African Americans more equal opportunities particularly in education and employment

ACTIVITY

The following were all aims of various civil rights groups of the 1960s. For each one, decide how far that aim was achieved and the reasons why.

- An end to 'Jim Crow' laws – legal segregation
- An end to segregation in practice
- An end to barriers preventing African Americans from voting
- An increase in African American voters
- Improved access to jobs
- Improved housing, living conditions, etc.

RECAP

RECALL QUIZ

1 What is meant by the term 'sit-in'?
2 Who was 'Bull' Connor and why is he significant to civil rights protests?
3 What were the SCLC and SNCC?
4 Outline the terms of the 1964 Civil Rights Act and 1965 Voting Act.
5 Explain the methods of protest used by Martin Luther King.
6 What happened in Selma in 1965?
7 Give three reasons for the growth of Black Power.
8 Who was Stokely Carmichael?
9 Who founded the Black Panthers?
10 Give three consequences of the race riots of 1964–68.

CHECKPOINT

STRENGTHEN
S1 What was the significance of the sit-ins and freedom rides?
S2 Explain the significance of the civil rights legislation of the 1960s.
S3 To what extent do you believe the Freedom Summer was a failure?

CHALLENGE
C1 What was Malcolm X's contribution to the civil rights movement?
C2 Was the civil rights legislation of the 1960s due to the protests of the civil rights movement?
C3 Explain the impact of Black Power on the civil rights movement.

SUMMARY

- In 1960, the first sit-in was staged in Greensboro, North Carolina. It started a mainly student-driven mass movement across many towns and cities, and forced some facilities to integrate.
- Freedom rides were organised to test whether bus facilities had been desegregated. They often met with extreme violence, including the Anniston bombing. The publicity forced the government to enforce the desegregation of bus facilities.
- In 1962, President Kennedy had to intervene to stop riots so that James Meredith could attend the University of Mississippi, as the Supreme Court had ruled he should.
- During a peace march in Birmingham, Alabama in 1963, the violent reaction from the police created huge publicity. This was followed by the huge March on Washington.
- His 'Dream' speech during the March on Washington fixed Martin Luther King as the leader of the civil rights movement.
- The Civil Rights Act was finally signed in 1964. This was followed by the signing of the Voting Rights Act in 1965 after the Freedom Summer and 'Bloody Sunday' at Selma.
- Malcolm X took a more confrontational approach to civil rights and believed that white people were the enemy. He argued that people should defend themselves if they were attacked.
- The Black Power movement was inspired by views such as Malcolm X's and by frustration with the slow progress of the civil rights movement. Stokely Carmichael is the person most associated with the phrase 'Black Power'.
- The Black Panthers were a Black Power group that retaliated against violence. They also set up projects to help African Americans in ghettos.
- There were major race riots across the USA during 1964–68. These were a response to poverty in the ghettos (due to discrimination and segregation) and unfair treatment by police and city officials.

EXAM GUIDANCE: PART (C) QUESTIONS

A01   **A02**

SKILLS PROBLEM SOLVING, REASONING, DECISION MAKING, ADAPTIVE LEARNING, INNOVATION

Question to be answered: 'The main achievement of the civil rights movement was that it increased awareness of the unfair ways that African Americans were treated.'

How far do you agree? Explain your answer.

You may use the following in your answer:
- **awareness of the treatment of African Americans**
- **the Civil Rights Act (1964).**

You must also use information of your own.   (16 marks)

1 **Analysis Question 1: What is the question type testing?**
In this question you have to demonstrate that you have knowledge and understanding of the key features and characteristics of the period studied. In this particular case, you need to show knowledge and understanding of the achievements of the civil rights movement.

You also have to explain, analyse and make judgements about historical events and periods to give an explanation and reach a judgement on the significance of something. In this particular case, you must consider the achievements of the civil rights movement.

2 **Analysis Question 2: What do I have to do to answer the question well?**
You have been given two topics to write about: the increased awareness of the unfair way that African Americans were treated and the Civil Rights Act (1964). You don't have to use the stimulus material provided but you will find it hard to assess the achievement of increasing awareness of the unfair ways that African Americans were treated if you don't write about it! You must avoid just giving the information. You also have to say why and how whatever you choose was an achievement.

You are also asked to consider whether the increased awareness of the unfair way that African Americans were treated was the main achievement, so you are going to need to compare achievements. You have been given the Civil Rights Act (1964) as another achievement, but the question says you must use information of your own. So you should include at least one more achievement, other than those you have been given. This achievement might be the Voting Rights Act (1965) or an increased pride in African American history and culture. If you include one of those, you will have three achievements to explain.

3 **Analysis Question 3: Are there any techniques I can use to make it very clear that I am doing what is needed to be successful?**
This is a 16-mark question and you need to make sure you give a substantial answer. You will be up against time pressures so try using some of these techniques to help you succeed.
- Only give a brief introduction, which answers the question straight away and shows what your paragraphs are going to be about.

■ Try to use the words of the question at the beginning of each paragraph. This will help you to stay focused on the question and avoid writing narrative.

■ Remember this question is a significance question. Make sure your answer explains how and why this was an achievement.

■ Don't simply state which achievement was most significant. Make sure you explain your choice by comparing the different achievements.

In summary, to score high marks on this question you need to do three things: provide coverage of content range (at least three achievements); provide coverage of arguments for and against the statement; provide clear reasons (criteria) for an overall judgement, backed by convincing argument.

Answer
Here is a student response to the question. The teacher has made some comments.

This introduction is far too long and goes into unnecessary detail. You need to make a 'crisp' start, so you could end the introduction after the third sentence and add the information on the Civil Rights Act into the paragraph where civil rights are discussed.

The civil rights movement did increase awareness of the unfair ways that African Americans were treated. This was a significant achievement of the civil rights movement because it helped lead to change that brought about greater equality. However, I believe that the Civil Rights Act of 1964 was the main achievement of the movement because it effectively ended segregation and, although it could not make sure that discrimination ended, it did make it illegal. The Civil Rights Act did not just happen because of the civil rights movement, however, it took the hard work of President Johnson in getting it passed and the people in Congress who approved it too. The act banned segregation and discrimination in public places and established the Equal Opportunities Commission to investigate discrimination in the workplace. These were very significant because segregation was widespread, particularly in the Southern states of the USA, and African Americans faced frequent discrimination in employment throughout the whole country.

Good paragraph. Answers the question, gives contextual knowledge and shows how the civil rights movement raised awareness and why this was significant.

The civil rights movement increased awareness of the unfair ways that African Americans were treated by the different kinds of protest that were organised. For example, sit-ins, that first began in Greensboro in 1960, highlighted the different facilities such as lunch counters, restaurants, beaches and parks that were segregated so African Americans had to use separate facilities from white people. The facilities for African Americans were often much poorer than the ones for whites. Many of the protests provoked a violent reaction from racists, which added to the publicity and helped to highlight the violence that African Americans often had to face. Increasing awareness was significant because many white people, especially in the North, were unaware of the extreme segregation and racism of the South, leading to increased pressure for change.

This paragraph really needs more on why the Civil Rights Act was the main achievement of the civil rights movement. Moving some of the information from the introduction to here would help.

This is disappointing. Although you have identified another achievement of the civil rights movement, there should be some detail on how the civil rights movement helped bring about the Voting Rights Act, what the act actually said and why this was significant.

Good, concise finish, although you could mention the Voting Rights Act here as that's the other example you've used in the answer.

However, raising awareness did not necessarily bring about change so I think that the Civil Rights Act is the main achievement of the civil rights movement. The protests of the civil rights movement put pressure on congress and the president to take action to make segregation and discrimination illegal. Even though the Civil Rights Act didn't end discrimination, as it was difficult to enforce, it made sure that legal segregation (the Jim Crow laws) ended and there was more chance of prosecuting people and businesses that discriminated against African Americans.

Another significant achievement of the civil rights movement was the Voting Rights Act of 1965, which led to more African Americans voting, which was important because then politicians would have to take more notice of issues that impacted on African Americans.

In conclusion, the main achievement of the civil rights movement was the Civil Rights Act of 1964 as this ended legal segregation, which had been prevalent throughout the South for 100 years. Although raising awareness of the unfair treatment African Americans received was important, it did not bring about as much change as the Civil Rights Act did.

What are the strengths and weaknesses of this answer?
You can see the strengths and weaknesses of this answer from what the teacher says. It would not take much to turn this into a very good answer – a shorter introduction and more detail in places, especially on the Voting Rights Act.

Work with a friend
Discuss with a friend how you would rewrite the weaker paragraphs in the answer to enable the whole answer to get very high marks.

Use the Student Book to set a part (c) question for a friend. Then look at the answer. Does it do the following things?

Answer checklist
☐ Identifies achievements
☐ Provides detailed information to support the achievements
☐ Shows which of the achievements was most significant
☐ Discusses factors other than those given in the question
☐ Addresses the 'main reason' by looking at arguments for and against and comparing them.

4. OTHER PROTEST MOVEMENTS: STUDENTS, WOMEN, ANTI-VIETNAM

LEARNING OBJECTIVES

- Understand reasons for the growth of protest movements
- Understand the links between student protest and the anti-Vietnam War movement
- Understand the women's movement and opposition to it.

Many people were inspired by the successes of the civil rights movement and the 1960s saw the growth of many other protest movements as people tried to make their voices heard.

Students campaigned on a wide range of issues, joining other protests for greater equality for African Americans and women, as well as forming their own protest groups to protest against the rules and policies of their universities and the government. The hippy movement, calling for a counter-culture of peace, free-love, music and drugs, shocked many older people but had a big impact on the young. The student protests had a huge variety of aims and opinions, but they were united by opposition to the Vietnam War.

Women also began to protest for greater rights and equality. The more moderate protestors wanted to end discrimination against women and wanted equal pay for equal work. The more radical protestors in the women's liberation movement wanted a complete change of society. The issue that most divided US society was abortion; as feminist protests began to have an impact on abortion laws, there was a huge backlash and opposition to the women's movement.

4.1 REASONS FOR THE GROWTH OF PROTEST MOVEMENTS

LEARNING OBJECTIVES

- Understand the influence of the civil rights movement on other groups
- Understand other shared reasons for the growth of protest movements in the 1960s
- Understand that there were also specific reasons for the growth of each protest movement.

The civil rights movement was not the only protest movement of the 1960s in the USA. Various other groups, including students and women, set up protest movements to try and change society. There were several reasons why these movements developed.

THE IMPACT OF CIVIL RIGHTS PROTESTS

Many young people, both black and white, had taken part in the civil rights protests. The sit-ins of 1960–61 were effectively the first student protest of the 1960s (see pages 43–45). Young people used their experience of civil rights protests to organise more protests, using similar methods, to highlight other parts of society they were unhappy with. The civil rights movement also inspired other groups, who believed they were facing similar prejudice and discrimination. These included women and ethnic groups such as Hispanic Americans and, later, Native Americans.

EXTRACT A

From an article in a women's magazine, published in 1995.

During the fifties and early sixties, the civil rights movement captured the public imagination and educated it on the immorality of discrimination and the legitimacy of mass protest. As such, it became the mother of all the movements of the sixties and seventies.

DISAPPOINTMENT AND DISILLUSIONMENT

US society changed during the Second World War. For example, more women went out to work. When the war ended, many people hoped that society would continue to change and become more equal. Instead, the 1950s largely saw a return to the pre-war situation. White men seemed to be the only group who were experiencing wealth, and many people were angered by the lack of change and the unfairness of society.

The election of the young, dynamic President Kennedy in 1960 seemed to offer the promise of change. His assassination in 1963, before he was able to fulfil his policies, shocked and depressed many Americans. Kennedy's death may well explain why there so much protest in American society from 1963.

THE EMERGENCE OF THE TEENAGER

Before the 1950s, most young people behaved as their parents did. During the 1950s, however, more people in their teens rebelled against their parents and began to question their parents' beliefs and values. A separate culture for young people emerged, with musicians such as Elvis Presley and films such as *Rebel without a Cause*, starring James Dean. As these 'teenagers' entered the 1960s and went to college, they continued to question the actions and beliefs of their parents' society and started to form and join protest groups.

THE MEDIA

Though other forms of media such as newspapers continued to be popular, the 1960s saw a huge rise in television viewers. For the first time, most American homes had televisions and saw what was happening thousands of kilometres away from the USA. The Vietnam War received huge coverage from all types of media from 1965 and this led to a growth in opposition to the war. Media coverage of the protests themselves also attracted more supporters to their causes but it also led to a growth of opposition to some of those movements. Television coverage of issues such as racism also raised awareness and led to people joining and starting protests.

THE INCREASING ROLE OF GOVERNMENT

In the 1930s, President Roosevelt's Democratic government had made many changes to try and help those suffering in the **Great Depression**. Since then, it had become increasingly accepted that the Federal government could, and should, intervene to solve problems and improve society. Before this, fighting injustice was not really seen as the government's role. By the 1960s, many Americans expected their Federal government to help those in need and take measures to make people's lives better. This inspired people to protest to ask the government to take action in order to tackle recognised injustices.

ACTIVITY

1 Create a ladder of reasons why protest movements grew in the 1960s, with the most important reason at the top.
2 Read Extract A. How does it suggest the civil rights movement inspired other groups to protest?

OTHER FACTORS

Various other factors played a role in inspiring protest movements in 1960s America.
- After the Second World War there was an increase in the birth rate. So by the 1960s the 'baby boomers' (as people born at this time were called) made up a large percentage of the population. Society had to start listening to the views of the young, because there were so many of them.
- **Music and the arts.** Many ideas that led to protests were communicated through the art and music of the time. Singers such as Bob Dylan, Jimi Hendrix and Janis Joplin and bands such as the Beatles and Country Joe and the Fish promoted alternative life styles which challenged American traditions.
- **Economic prosperity.** By the 1960s, there was great prosperity in the USA, but this was overwhelmingly for white **Protestant** men. The greater wealth of these people highlighted those who were not so fortunate.
- **Protest movements elsewhere in the world.** During the 1960s, there were many protest movements across the world, not just in the USA. For example, the protests in Paris in May 1968 saw huge demonstrations, and workers went on strike in protest against capitalism and traditional values. Protests such as these inspired people to protest in other countries, including the USA.

SPECIFIC FACTORS

The factors mentioned above (which applied to much of society) happened at the same time as a series of events that encouraged specific parts of society to protest. For example, the invention of the contraceptive pill and the increasing availability of time-saving domestic appliances (such as washing machines) led more women to question their roles in society (see page 86). For students, the factors mentioned above led to an increased awareness of the unfairness (as they saw it) of some of the rules of the universities they attended (see page 75). For many Americans, particularly young people, it was the horrors of the conflict in Vietnam, and US actions within that war, that inspired them to protest (see page 79).

EXAM-STYLE QUESTION

A01   **A02**

SKILLS PROBLEM SOLVING, REASONING, DECISION MAKING, ADAPTIVE LEARNING, INNOVATION

'Television was the main reason for the explosion of protest movements in the USA in the 1960s.'

How far do you agree? Explain your answer.

You may use the following in your answer:
- television
- the civil rights movement.

You **must** also use information of your own.   **(16 marks)**

HINT

Whether you agree or disagree with the statement, you will need to explore a range of other reasons for the growth of protest movements in your answer, including reasons specific to each protest movement.

4.2 STUDENT PROTESTS

LEARNING OBJECTIVES

- ☐ Understand the role of Students for a Democratic Society and the Berkeley Free Speech Movement in student protests
- ☐ Understand the anti-Vietnam War movement and the role of students within these protests
- ☐ Understand the hippy movement.

After the Second World War, there was a rapid rise in the number of Americans going to college. By 1970, nearly 40 per cent of all young people (and there were a lot of young people due to the post-war baby boom) went on to higher education after leaving school. The majority of these students were from white, middle-class backgrounds, and their parents expected them to think and behave just as they had done: to conform with society and support the government. Traditionally, American universities had been places where students concentrated on their studies, and enjoyed their sport and social life. They were not usually places where political and social issues generated much interest. However, during the 1960s, students became increasingly concerned with major social issues and the injustices that existed in American society.

Throughout the 1960s and 1970s, students actively campaigned on a huge variety of issues including civil rights for African Americans and other ethnic groups, gay rights, women's rights, poverty, US foreign policy, **nuclear disarmament** and the environment. They joined existing protests and organisations, such as CORE and the SNCC, and also set up their own organisations to protest against government policies or those of the college they were attending.

Many students rejected the views and opinions of older people, including their parents; they felt that these people had helped to create a **corrupt** society that treated people unfairly. A popular **slogan** during student protests was 'Don't trust anyone over 30'. Most student activists were left-wing, believing that the government should actively be involved in improving the lives of its citizens. However, they also wanted to see direct involvement by citizens to demonstrate their views and work to improve things – it was not enough to

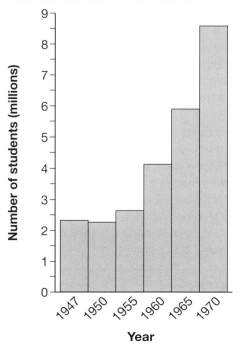

SOURCE A

Student enrolment in American universities, 1947–70, from official statistics.

KEY TERMS

right-wing conservative views that value tradition and the freedom of the individual, so the role of government is minimal

conservative not liking changes or new ideas

just vote for an official in elections. There were many students who rejected this radical approach and supported the traditional **right-wing, conservative** attitude to education and government, but their voices were much less influential at this time.

There were so many diverse student causes that critics of the movement claimed that students just wanted to rebel against anything they saw as part of their parent's society and beliefs, without understanding the issues fully. There was, of course, an element of truth in this, but most students believed that society itself was the problem. Many referred to society as 'the machine' or 'the system' (see Source D).

SOURCE B

From an interview with a student protestor in 1970.

I reject everything my father stands for. I do not want to gear my life to making money. I do not want to get ahead. I do not have his patriotism for a nation that can't behave decently. I don't believe in the military, the Republican Party or the First National Bank.

STUDENTS FOR A DEMOCRATIC SOCIETY

SOURCE C

A sit-in organised by Students for a Democratic Society in the administration building of Queens College, City University New York, 16 April 1969.

One of the first protest organisations set up by students was Students for a Democratic Society. Its first meeting was held in 1960 at the University of Michigan. After a meeting in 1962, it released the Port Huron Statement, which explained that its aims were to campaign against 'racial injustice, war and the violation of human rights'.

Many members of SDS took part in the civil rights sit-ins and freedom rides of 1961–62. Its first focus as an organisation, however, was on campaigning for

better student rights within universities and colleges. It organised sit-ins and **rallies** to try and give students more say in the policies and practices of the universities (such as the courses offered). The SDS also protested against the rules that allowed university officials to act like the students' parents by setting strict rules – for example, saying what time students had to return to their accommodation in the evening.

The SDS began as a small organisation, but it grew throughout the 1960s. By the end of the decade, 150 colleges or universities across the USA had SDS groups, with a total of 100,000 members. Membership dramatically increased in 1966 because of opposition to the Vietnam War (see pages 79–81).

THE BERKELEY FREE SPEECH MOVEMENT

The protests at the University of California in Berkeley, in the autumn of 1964, brought a lot of media attention and made many Americans aware of the student movement. Some of the volunteers who took part in the Mississippi Freedom Summer (see pages 53–54) were students at Berkeley as well

SOURCE D

From a speech by Mario Savio, leader of the Free Speech Movement at the University of California, Berkeley, 2 December 1964.

There is a time when the operation of the machine becomes so odious [unpleasant], makes you so sick at heart, that you can't take part; you can't even passively take part and you've got to put your bodies upon the gears and upon the wheels, upon the levers, upon all the apparatus and you've got to make it stop. And you've got to indicate to the people who run it, to the people who own it, that unless you're free, the machine will be prevented from working at all.

as being members of SDS. When they returned for the new semester in September 1964, they organised protests against racial discrimination on the university campus. The university administration responded by banning students from protesting on university grounds for 'off campus political and social action'.

The students ignored the ban and carried on protesting. A few of them were suspended by the university, so the remaining students, around 400 of them, signed a petition and filled the hall of the administration building, demanding that they too should be suspended. Police were called and they arrested one of the protestors, Jack Weinberg. But the police car was blocked for 32 hours by students who refused to move and made speeches criticising the university. More police were brought in and threatened to arrest all the protestors, but students negotiated with the university's president and agreed to leave.

After this, students created the Free Speech Movement in order to protest and negotiate until they won what they saw as their right to hold protests and speak about anything they wanted to on university grounds. Weinberg and Mario Savio (who had impressed his fellow students with his speeches during the earlier protest) were leading members of the movement, which included a wide variety of student groups. Members of the FSM included those with conservative and **moderate** views as well as those with radical ideas.

The FSM produced thousands of leaflets and held many meetings and rallies to gain support. Members made badges and Christmas cards to fund the campaign; they also asked for donations. At its peak, nearly 14,000 (around half) of Berkeley's students supported the FSM's campaign.

At the end of November, however, despite being told they would not be punished, four of the students who had originally been suspended were charged with breaking university rules in leading the earlier protests. In response, the FSM organised a rally and sit-in of the administration building on 2 December, which was supported by around 6,000 students. Police arrested the protestors, but it took them 12 hours to make 750 arrests, as the students refused to leave.

SOURCE E

Mario Savio, a founder of the Free Speech Movement, speaks at a rally at the Univeristy of California, Berkeley.

ACTIVITY

'The Free Speech Movement was completely successful in its protests at the University of California.' Explain whether or not you agree with this statement.

A few days later, university staff voted strongly in favour for there to be no limits on the protests allowed on the campus. On the face of it, the Free Speech Movement had won, and students were allowed to use university grounds for political protests and debates. However, there were very detailed rules about how, when and where protests could be carried out. The students who had been arrested were all convicted and fined. The leaders were sentenced to between 1 and 4 months in prison.

THE ACHIEVEMENTS OF THE STUDENT MOVEMENT

SOURCE F

Members of the Free Speech Movement taking part in the sit-in on 2 December 1964.

In many ways, the Berkeley Free Speech Movement demonstrates the problems encountered by the wider student movement. As the FSM became more confrontational, it lost the support of many moderate students. It also never had much support in the local community. Many people were appalled at the students' behaviour, especially after a swear word was used on signs at a rally. This led to the FSM being labelled the 'Filthy Speech Movement' by those who disapproved. Indeed, unlike the African American civil rights movement, the student movement never gained more general support in US society. Many older people regarded the protesting students as troublemakers who had nothing better to do.

As at Berkeley, the student protests often achieved some of their aims with regards to students' rights at college, but few of their other aims were really met. Part of the problem was the huge variety of issues they were protesting about and the numerous differing views within the student movement. However, there was one issue that united the student movement – opposition to the Vietnam War.

EXAM-STYLE QUESTION

A01   **A02**

Explain **two** effects of the student movement on the USA.   **(8 marks)**

HINT

You can include the anti-Vietnam War protests on pages 80–82 in this answer if you wish.

THE VIETNAM WAR

Throughout the 1950s, tensions between communist North Vietnam and the strongly anti-communist government of South Vietnam increased. During the Cold War (see Section 1.2), US presidents were desperate to prevent South Vietnam becoming communist, because they believed this would encourage other countries in South Asia to adopt communism and support the Soviet Union. The USA sent advisers, supplies and money to support South Vietnam. In 1959, the situation turned into war. Angered by the actions of South Vietnam's government, the North sent soldiers into the South to help southern communists (known as Vietcong) take over the country.

US support for South Vietnam increased under President Kennedy and then Johnson in the 1960s. In August 1964, North Vietnamese boats attacked American boats off the coast of Vietnam. This led to Congress passing the Gulf of Tonkin Resolution requested by President Johnson. This gave Johnson the power to do anything necessary to prevent attacks on US forces, without having to seek approval from Congress. At the start of 1965, US aeroplanes began bombing North Vietnam and US troops joined the war in the South. US involvement increased as the war developed. By 1969, half a million US soldiers were in Vietnam.

The Vietnam War proved to be an extremely difficult one for the USA. Eventually troops were pulled out by President Nixon in 1973. By the end of 1975, the whole of South Vietnam had fallen to the communist North.

KEY TERM

draft a system in which people are ordered to join the army, navy, etc., especially during a war

THE ANTI-VIETNAM WAR PROTESTS

A small number of people publically protested against US involvement in Vietnam from the start but, as US military action increased, so did opposition to it. Protestors objected to many aspects of the war, including:

- the huge cost of US intervention (paid for by American tax-payers), with little apparent success. As the war continued, more people realised that the USA could never win.
- the rising number of deaths and injuries to US troops
- US support of the corrupt government of South Vietnam, even if it was anti-communist
- the USA seemed to be acting like an **imperial power** by enforcing its will on people living in another country
- US tactics in Vietnam, including mass bombings and the use of chemical weapons such as Agent Orange to destroy crops and forests. These actions killed and injured many Vietnamese civilians
- the **draft** system, which was seen as very unfair. It meant that most soldiers were very young (the average age was just 21, compared to an average age of 26 for US soldiers in the Second World War) and a high percentage of African Americans and poor whites were drafted because they were less likely to go to college (students were exempt from the draft).

By the end of 1965, the anti-war movement was starting to generate publicity and gather force. In October, the SDS publically declared its objection to the war and almost immediately its membership began to rise dramatically. At this stage, most protestors were students and other young people.

EXTEND YOUR KNOWLEDGE

CONTROVERSIAL TACTICS IN VIETNAM
Many of the tactics used by the USA in Vietnam, such as mass bombings and forcibly moving Vietnamese civilians from their villages to live in camps, were very controversial. Over 4.5 million acres of land was sprayed with Agent Orange, which destroyed the forest and animals that lived there as well as causing health problems for people. The events at My Lai on 16 March 1968 probably caused the most public anger. US troops found no Vietcong in the village of My Lai, but still massacred all the women, children and old men. It was later found that the troops were following the orders of their superiors, who later tried to hide their orders and knowledge of the massacre.

ACTIVITY

1 Discuss why most anti-Vietnam war protestors were young people.
2 Read Source G. What reasons does the source give for opposing the Vietnam War? How do you think someone supporting the war would respond to it?

SOURCE G

From the Students for a Democratic Society *Guide to Conscientious Objection*, October 1965.

We feel that the war is immoral at its root, that it is fought alongside a regime with no claim to represent its people, and that it is foreclosing [cutting off] the hope of making America a decent and truly democratic society. The commitment of the SDS, and of the whole generation we represent, is clear: we are anxious to build villages; we refuse to burn them. We are anxious to help and to change our country; we refuse to destroy someone else's country. We are anxious to advance the cause of democracy; we do not believe that cause can be advanced by torture and terror.

The media played a part in creating opposition to the war as news reporters and cameras had access to the conflict and were allowed to broadcast what they wanted. For the first time, Americans could see the horrors of war for themselves on television. Footage of burning villages and terrified and injured children increased support for the anti-war movement, as well as damaging the USA's reputation abroad. As the war continued, the protestors came from more diverse backgrounds. Increasing numbers of older people and some returning soldiers joined the campaign, forming groups such as Veterans and Reservists to End the War and Vets for Peace.

THE PROTESTS

Anti-war campaigners used the methods of the civil rights movement and student movement, as well as coming up with some new ideas to demonstrate their objections to US involvement in Vietnam. Protests included:

■ mass rallies, where protestors shouted slogans such as 'Hey, hey, LBJ, how many kids did you kill today?' (LBJ being the initials of President Johnson) and 'Hell no, we won't go!'. They also joked about senior soldiers, for example, by dressing up as General 'Wastemoreland' to insult the commander of US forces in Vietnam, General Westmoreland.
■ sit-ins and/or teach-ins, where people gave lectures on the conflict in Vietnam. These protests were held in public buildings, in army recruitment centres and even on the railway tracks transporting troops
■ burning draft cards and helping those who had been drafted to go into hiding or leave the USA, as well as giving advice on how to avoid the draft in the first place.

The protests peaked between 1968 and 1970. In the first 6 months of 1968, there were 100 anti-war demonstrations across the country. The largest individual protest was a march on Washington in November 1969, which attracted over 500,000 supporters. As with other protests, some anti-war demonstrations turned violent and there were frequent fights with police. At Kent State University in Ohio, national guardsmen were called to break up a protest on 4 May 1970. The students refused to move despite tear gas being used, so the troops fired into the crowd. Four students were killed and 11 injured. Two weeks later, two African American students were shot and killed by police trying to break up a protest at Jackson State University. Many Americans were extremely shocked.

EXTEND YOUR KNOWLEDGE

PROTEST MUSIC

The events at Kent State University, Ohio were cast into American memory largely thanks to the song 'Ohio' by supergroup Bing Crosby, Stephen Stills, Graham Nash and Neil Young. Young wrote the lyrics after seeing the photos of the shootings and they included blaming President Nixon for the death of the students. The song was banned from some radio stations. There were also many songs written in protest against Vietnam, such as Country Joe and the Fish's 'I feel like I'm fixin' to die', Barry McGuire's 'Eve of destruction' and John Lennon's 'Give peace a chance'. The latter was sung by half a million people during the Moratorium march on Washington (a protest against the Vietnam War) in November 1969.

SOURCE H

Teenager Mary Ann Vecchio kneels over the body of student Jeffrey Miller during an anti-war demonstration at Kent State University, Ohio, 4 May 1970.

SOURCE I

A cartoon from a British newspaper, published on 15 October 1969.

"No irresponsible demonstrators are going to tell me how to run the United States!"

THE IMPACT OF THE ANTI-VIETNAM WAR MOVEMENT

KEY TERM

Vietnamization Nixon's policy from mid-1969, to help South Vietnam's government take more responsibility for the war and use more Vietnamese troops rather than Americans

It is difficult to assess the impact of the anti-war movement. It undoubtedly helped to split society into those who supported the war and those who did not. Many historians believe the protests were a major reason why President Johnson chose not to stand for re-election in 1968 and why Richard Nixon was elected instead of his Democrat opponent. The protests did put pressure on the government and raised awareness of anti-war beliefs, and they may have been a reason for Nixon's policy of **Vietnamization**. However, it is not clear whether they had much impact on ending US involvement in Vietnam; it is likely that the government would have withdrawn from the war even without the protests.

Although the anti-Vietnam War movement did persuade increasing numbers of people to support its cause, many Americans did not trust the protesters. They were seen as unpatriotic, especially as some anti-war protesters burned the US flag and openly declared their support for North Vietnam and communism. Some Americans, including some students, strongly supported the war and held pro-war rallies and demonstrations. President Nixon expressed his belief that the 'silent majority' of Americans supported his policies and did not openly protest either for or against the war. Some opinion polls seemed to prove him right, as more people approved than disapproved of his handling of the Vietnam War.

ACTIVITY

1 What is the message of Source I?
2 List some similarities and differences between civil rights protests and the student protests.

HIPPIES

KEY TERM

commune a group of people who live together and share the work and their possessions

While many young people protested through the student protests and anti-war movement, others chose to reject society altogether by 'dropping out'. These people were known as hippies. Hippies chose not to work or go to college. Many lived in **communes** in cities such as San Francisco, while others travelled around living out of buses or vans. They created a counter-culture to traditional America with different moral codes that promoted peace, love and happiness. Their slogans included 'make love, not war' and 'if it feels good, do it'. They experimented with sex, drugs and various forms of art, especially music. Rock music was central to hippies' lives and, for many, the crown of the hippy movement was the Woodstock music festival in August 1969, where up to half a million people gathered.

Hippies tended to have long, un-styled hair and wore very colourful clothes and jewellery. Nakedness was also encouraged when the weather allowed. Many wore flowers and handed them out to people, including police and soldiers, which led to hippies being called 'flower children'. Their emphasis on peace and love, however, did not mean that hippies were passive. Because of their strong anti-war views and belief in racial and gender equality, they were passionately involved in civil rights, women's rights and anti-Vietnam War protests. Many also campaigned on environmental issues.

SOURCE J

Hippies in El Rito, New Mexico in 1969.

EXTRACT B

From an article about the cause and effect of the 1960s hippy movement.

Because of hippies' sexual openness, alternative lifestyles such as homosexuality and transexuality are generally more accepted. Young adults have become more sexually active at a younger age because of the influence of past generations. Overall, the hippie movement was a time of not only exploring oneself and rebelling against society, but it was also a time of acceptance. After the hippie movement, African Americans, working women, homosexuals, nudity and non-traditional apparel [clothing] all became generally more accepted. Without the hippie movement, the United States would not be as free and adoptive as it is today. The 1960s was a highly influential time and the hippies were highly influential people.

THE IMPACT OF THE HIPPY MOVEMENT

Many Americans were very shocked by the hippy movement. They viewed hippies as 'wasters' and could not understand why their children wanted to behave in this way and reject the society their parents had helped to create. For them, hippies were corrupting and harming their country. It is perhaps unsurprising then that, with the exception of the advances made in civil rights for African Americans and women, hippies had little impact on government policies.

However, hippies did have a lasting impact on society. Although few young people actually became hippies themselves, many adopted some aspects of the movement, such as wearing unusual clothes, listening to rock music, and experimenting with drugs and sex. Hippy ideas of equality, individuality and tolerance of everyone no matter what their sexuality, race or gender did eventually help these things to become more acceptable to wider US society.

EXAM-STYLE QUESTION

AO4

SKILLS ANALYSIS, INTERPRETATION, CREATIVITY

Study Extract B.

What impression does the author give about the impact of hippies on the USA?

You **must** use Extract B to explain your answer. **(6 marks)**

HINT

Remember that you can annotate the extract to help you break it down and understand what the author means.

4.3 THE WOMEN'S MOVEMENT

LEARNING OBJECTIVES

- Understand the contributions of Eleanor Roosevelt, Betty Friedan and NOW to the women's movement
- Understand the more radical aims of the Women's Liberation Movement and the issue of abortion
- Understand the role of Phyllis Schlafly and opposition to the women's movement.

The two world wars had expanded female job opportunities and increased the number of women in the workforce. However, by 1960, most Americans still believed that a woman's primary role was to look after the home and raise children. When women married, it was expected that they would give up their jobs and become housewives. Some companies even dismissed female employees once they got married.

SOURCE K

1950s advertisements, such as this one for a refrigerator, were often focused on a housewife and mother, demonstrating the views of the time.

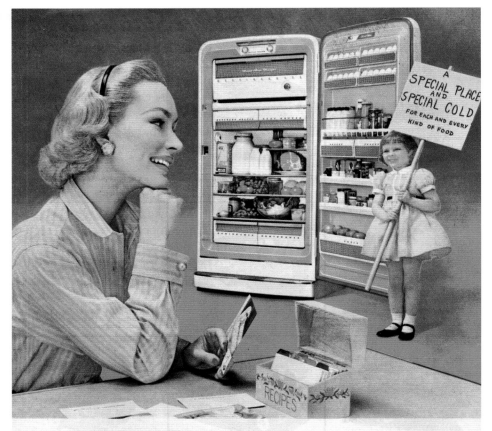

A SPECIAL PLACE AND SPECIAL COLD FOR EACH AND EVERY KIND OF FOOD

If you like a well-organized kitchen...
you'll love the new Westinghouse Food File Refrigerator

It's an entirely New Kind of Refrigerator with a SPECIAL PLACE and SPECIAL COLD for each and every kind of food! Yes, just as you file your recipes . . . now you can file your food where you can find it easily and quickly. For this new Westinghouse Refrigerator gives you 100% *organized* storage space for any type of food . . . frozen, cooked or fresh . . . with the right cold to keep it safely.

It's FROST-FREE, of course. No defrosting to do in the Freezer or in the Refrigerator . . . no messy defrost water to empty EVER!

See TV's Top Dramatic Show . . . Westinghouse Studio One . . . Every Week

Giant Freezer . . . Holds 56 lbs. frozen foods in safe zero-cold.
Exclusive Beverage Keeper . . . Just the right cold for all beverages.
Meat Keeper . . . Keeps up to 18 lbs. of meat butcher-fresh.
Roll-Out Shelves . . . Bring foods out front, in sight, in reach.
Cheese File . . . holds 2-lb. package at proper temperature and moisture.

Butter Keeper . . . Keeps butter just right for easy spreading.
4 Egg Keepers . . . Lift out one or two eggs, or remove entire section.
Two Big Humidrawers . . . Keep more than ⅗-bu. vegetables garden-fresh.
Fruit Bin . . . Holds quantities of fruits in door, at your finger tips.
Snack Keeper . . . Stores candy, sandwiches, canapes and tidbits.

YOU CAN BE SURE . . . IF IT'S Westinghouse

WESTINGHOUSE ELECTRIC CORPORATION, ELECTRIC APPLIANCE DIVISION, MANSFIELD, OHIO

ELEANOR ROOSEVELT

One influential campaigner for improved rights and opportunities for women between 1933 and 1962 was **First Lady** Eleanor Roosevelt. She held her own press conferences, the first First Lady to do so, and allowed only women to attend. This meant that newspapers and radio stations had to employ female journalists. She also put pressure on her husband and later presidents to employ more women. Roosevelt made broadcasts on the radio and television and wrote many articles (including her own newspaper column) voicing her opinions on many matters including women's rights. Her work helped to increase support for women's rights and bring about legislation for more equality.

Eleanor Roosevelt was very influential in the Democratic Party. She agreed to support John Kennedy in his campaign to win the **nomination** for the Democrat's candidate for president only if he agreed to establish a commission on the status of women if he became president. As a result, he created the President's Commission on the Status of Women in December 1961 and appointed Roosevelt as chair, although she died before it reported its findings. The report highlighted the huge inequalities facing women in work, finding that women were overwhelmingly in low-paid jobs with few responsibilities. Only four per cent of lawyers and seven per cent of doctors were women. Women earned between 50 and 60 per cent of what a man earned for doing the same job and had very few opportunities for progression in their careers.

SOURCE L

Federal employment statistics for April 1962, which show that women were mostly in the lower-paid jobs.

EXTEND YOUR KNOWLEDGE

ELEANOR ROOSEVELT'S ACHIEVEMENTS

Eleanor Roosevelt was internationally admired and respected as a diplomat and human rights campaigner. As a delegate to the United Nations, she helped to write the Universal Declaration of Human Rights. She also campaigned for racial equality and the Ku Klux Klan apparently put a price on her head. In 1938, when attending a meeting in Birmingham, Alabama, she ignored segregation laws by sitting beside an African American. When asked to move, she asked for a ruler to measure the gap between the black and white seating areas and sat directly in the middle of the gap.

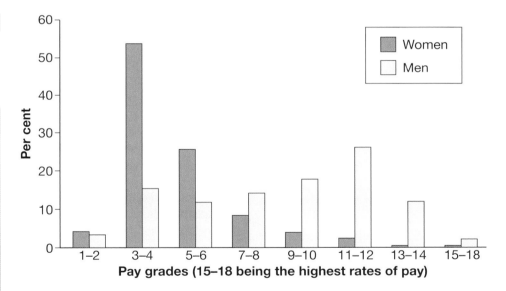

Partly as a result of the Commission's Report, the Equal Pay Act was signed by President Kennedy in June 1963. This made it illegal to pay people different rates for doing the same job. It was followed by the Civil Rights Act of 1964 (see page 56), which made it illegal to discriminate against someone because of their gender.

FACTORS FOR CHANGE

EXTRACT C

From an interview with a historian in 2017.

Of course, other forms of contraception had been available for years. So when the pill was approved in 1960, there was nothing particularly revolutionary about its introduction (though it was much more convenient to use). What made the difference was that the pill was taken by women. They didn't have to rely on men using contraception any more. The women's movement was quick to realise just how important this was in giving women control of their own lives, and it was their work which meant things changed rapidly.

Several social and economic factors, which developed from the 1950s, had an impact on women's roles. By 1960, society had begun to place more value on gadgets (such as televisions) and appliances (such as washing machines). As a result, it became more necessary for households to have more than one wage earner, so they could afford all these things. Additionally, household appliances saved considerable time, so female householders had more time for paid employment.

One of the most important developments was the availability of the contraceptive pill from 1960. This helped women to plan when to have a family, which meant they could also plan their education and careers around this. However, access to the pill varied considerably across different states and for different women. It was not until 1965 that the Supreme Court ruled in *Griswold versus Connecticut* that all married women should be allowed to use birth control. In 1972, the Supreme Court extended the right to all women whatever their marital status. (Before this ruling, 26 states still banned unmarried women from accessing contraception).

These factors, along with the influence of other protest movements (especially the civil rights movement and hippies), helped women to achieve greater equality. However, many historians believe this greater equality would not have happened without the women's movement.

BETTY FRIEDAN

Despite Eleanor Roosevelt's influence, most historians credit another woman with starting the women's movement. Betty Friedan was a journalist who first came to prominence after the publication of her book, *The Feminine Mystique*, in 1963. The title of the book was the phrase Friedan used to describe what she found to be a myth: the idea that women should only find happiness and satisfaction in their role as housewives and mothers. At her college reunion in 1957, Friedan interviewed her fellow female graduates to ask whether they were happy with their lives. She also wrote articles on the same topic and received many letters from other women describing their feelings. The book explained Friedan's findings; that many well-educated and intelligent women were bored and unhappy with their role as housewives. She described these women's homes as comfortable prison camps, and pushed them to escape and find happiness in paid employment. She believed that women should have equal political, economic and social rights to men and that they should not be considered as suitable for only low-paid jobs. The book became a bestseller and was very influential in changing thinking in America.

ACTIVITY

1 List ways in which Eleanor Roosevelt helped to promote women's rights.
2 Begin a mind map of factors that helped to bring about greater equality for women. Add to it as you go through this section.

SOURCE M

From *The Feminine Mystique*, by Betty Friedan, published in 1963.

The problem lay buried, unspoken, for many years in the minds of American women. Each wife struggled with it alone. As she made the beds, shopped for groceries, matched furnishing fabric, ate peanut butter sandwiches with her children, drove them to Cub Scouts and Brownies, lay beside her husband at night – she was afraid to ask even herself the silent question 'Is this all?' There was no word of this feeling in all the novels, books and articles by experts telling women their role was to seek fulfilment as wives and mothers.

NOW

KEY TERM

feminist someone who believes that men and women should have equal rights and opportunities

▶ **Figure 4.1** NOW's Bill of Rights

ACTIVITY

Read NOW's Bill of Rights (Figure 4.1). Discuss each of the points in pairs or small groups. Sort the points in order of:

a those which you think would be easiest to enforce

b those which you think would be most to least controversial with Americans.

EXTEND YOUR KNOWLEDGE

NOW'S BILL OF RIGHTS TODAY

As of 2016, two points of NOW's Bill of Rights (numbers 1 and 5) have not been achieved at all, while the rest have only been achieved to some extent. For example, by Federal law, maternity rights are very limited. Women employed by a company with at least 50 employees are entitled to up to 12 weeks' unpaid leave after having a baby, during which time their jobs are protected. In only four US states are women entitled to paid maternity leave for 4 or 6 weeks depending on the state. By comparison, women in the UK are entitled to up to 52 weeks' maternity leave, of which up to 39 weeks' is paid.

KEY TERM

lobby (v) attempt to persuade a government to change a law, make a new law, etc.

The Equal Pay Act and Civil Rights Act were both important milestones. However, as African Americans were also discovering, new laws were not enough to end discrimination or change people's attitudes. Therefore, in June 1966, Betty Friedan and other **feminists** set up the National Organization for Women (NOW) as a **pressure group** to attract supporters and put pressure on the authorities to enforce equality. Friedan became its first president. In 1967, at its first national conference, it adopted a Bill of Rights setting out its aims (see Figure 4.1).

NOW's Bill of Rights

1 The Equal Rights Amendment to the Constitution is passed by Congress and ratified by states

2 Sex discrimination in employment, as set out in the Civil Rights Act of 1964, is enforced

3 Women's jobs to be protected after childbirth and maternity leave to be paid

4 Tax deductions for home and child care expenses for working parents

5 Child care facilities to be set up on the same basis as parks, libraries and schools

6 Discrimination and segregation by sex to be outlawed at all levels of education

7 Equal job training opportunities and access to welfare for women and men

8 Removal of laws limiting access to contraception and abortion

By 1970, NOW had approximately 40,000 members and worked on campaigns with a wide range of other groups, such as the National Women's Caucus and the Women's Campaign Fund. NOW used a variety of tactics to try and bring about change, including protest marches, strikes, petitions, **lobbying** politicians and taking legal action.

■ Between 1966 and 1971, NOW helped in a series of disputes about unequal pay and won $30 million in back pay for women.

■ On 26 August 1970, NOW organised the Women's Strike for Equality. Thousands of women across the USA went on strike to draw attention to unequal pay and discrimination in the workplace. The largest protest was a march down New York's Fifth Avenue in which an estimated 50,000 people took part.

■ In February 1970, members of NOW disrupted the Senate during a debate and displayed posters and boards calling for the Equal Rights Amendment (see page 91) to be discussed and passed.

abortion a medical operation to end a pregnancy so that the baby is not born alive

Women's Strike for Equality march, New York, 26 August 1970.

NOW helped to increase awareness of gender inequality and inspired many women to challenge the system, but it also had many critics. For some, it was too radical, particularly because of its support for the Equal Rights Amendment and **abortion**, whereas for others it was not radical enough. Moreover, NOW's supporters were mostly middle- or upper-class and well educated: some argued that it did little to improve the lives of poor women.

Explain **two** effects of the women's movement on the USA.   **(8 marks)**

You can use many pages within Section 4.3 to help you with this question, but remember to focus on just two effects.

WOMEN'S LIBERATION MOVEMENT

patriarchal where men hold the power and authority

lesbian a woman who is sexually attracted to other women

NOW was a moderate group within the women's movement. It wanted huge changes but within society as it was, with family units and marriage. The Women's **Liberation Movement** (or Women's Lib) is the name given to those feminists whose aims were far more radical. Supporters of Women's Liberation wanted to totally destroy the existing system and 'liberate' or free women from the limitations of **patriarchal** society. It included groups who wanted to completely separate women and men, and others who believed **lesbians** were the only women who could achieve true liberation. Some Women's Liberation groups regarded men as the enemy.

The methods of protest used by Women's Liberation groups were also different to more moderate groups. To begin with, their protests were aggressive. For example, they held sit-ins in company offices that created sexist advertisements and even damaged some offices. At the 1968 Miss America beauty contest in Atlantic City, radical feminists organised a protest against

EXTEND YOUR KNOWLEDGE

FEMINISTS AND BRA BURNING

Have you ever heard the phrase 'bra-burning feminist'? This began at the 1968 Miss America demonstration. Items such as make-up, copies of magazines with photographs of naked women, household cleaning tools and uncomfortable clothing (including bras) were thrown into a rubbish bin, but there's little evidence that bras were burned there. Some historians believe the myth grew because some reporters compared the protest to the burning of draft cards at anti-Vietnam War protests. Others believe it was created by those opposed to the women's movement who wanted to make feminists appear crazy. There are some reports of small protests where bras were burned later, probably inspired by the Miss America myth, but it never developed into a common thing.

the contest. They held boards, gave out leaflets, threw products that they felt showed that society only valued women for their looks into a rubbish bin and crowned a sheep Miss America. The protest attracted huge, mostly negative, media attention around the world, as well as within the USA.

The negative publicity attracted by their protests led many Women's Liberation groups to try a different approach. They tried to help women at a local level by setting up small discussion groups. In these groups, women explored their own experiences of things such as work, education, relationships and raising children. These groups helped to popularise the idea that the personal was political. This meant that even small steps made by individuals, such as how they dressed, helped to affect how all women were seen and treated by society. By 1974, these groups were also helping women to deal with issues such as rape and domestic violence.

SOURCE O

From an article in the *New York Post* about the Miss America protests, published on 12 September 1968.

As one who has always been on the side of protestors, I regret to say that I believe this demonstration in Atlantic City has gone too far… By demanding that women do away with all beauty aids, … these well-meaning but misled females were trying to destroy everything this country holds dear… It is a known fact that the American woman, beautiful though she is, needs all the help she can get…

ABORTION

SOURCE P

A protest in New York demonstrating in favour of abortion in 1973.

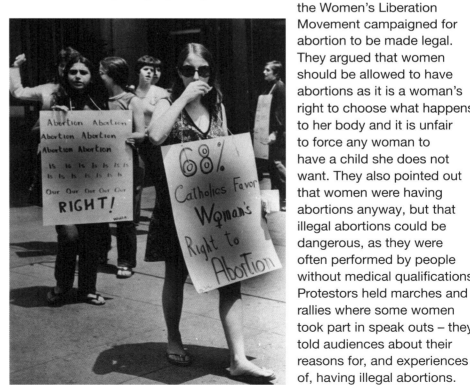

ACTIVITY

Abortion was, and still is, hugely controversial in the USA. Why do you think it is so controversial?

In 1960, abortion was illegal throughout the USA, unless the life of the mother was threatened by her pregnancy. Members of NOW and groups within the Women's Liberation Movement campaigned for abortion to be made legal. They argued that women should be allowed to have abortions as it is a woman's right to choose what happens to her body and it is unfair to force any woman to have a child she does not want. They also pointed out that women were having abortions anyway, but that illegal abortions could be dangerous, as they were often performed by people without medical qualifications. Protestors held marches and rallies where some women took part in speak outs – they told audiences about their reasons for, and experiences of, having illegal abortions.

EXTRACT D

From a book on Civil Rights, published in 2009.

The decision in the case of *Roe v. Wade* was a landmark in the history of the pursuit of women's rights... For the traditional defenders of home and family, it struck at the root of what they held most dear. It was almost certainly the most controversial, as well as the most significant event, since it was underpinned by arguments relating to a woman's right to control her own body and to make decisions on child bearing.

ROE VERSUS WADE

As more people campaigned, some states changed their abortion laws to allow an abortion in some circumstances, such as rape. In 1970, New York State changed the law to allow abortion on demand until the 24th week of pregnancy. Five other states (Alaska, California, Hawaii, Oregon and Washington) passed similar laws. Women's groups gave loans to help women who wanted abortions to travel to states where abortion was legal and to pay for the operation. In most states, however, abortion remained illegal except in cases where the mother's life was at risk.

In 1970, Norma McCorvey, under the name of Jane Roe, took the Dallas County District Attorney, Henry Wade, to court to claim the right to have an abortion. McCorvey had had her first two children adopted and she did not want to have another child. Roe's lawyers won, but the court ruled on this one case only, so they decided to appeal to the Supreme Court to try to make it a test case that would apply in all states for all women.

By seven votes to two, on 22 January 1973, the Supreme Court ruled that abortion laws broke a woman's constitutional right to privacy and freedom of personal choice in family matters (the Fourteenth Amendment). Some limitations were imposed, such as abortions being allowed after 6 months of pregnancy only if the woman's life was in danger. The case led to abortions becoming more available to women across the USA and most people in the Women's Movement saw it as a huge victory.

EXAM-STYLE QUESTION

A04

SKILLS   ANALYSIS, INTERPRETATION, CREATIVITY

Study Extract D.
What impression does the author give about the *Roe versus Wade* decision?

You **must** use Extract D to explain your answer.   **(6 marks)**

HINT

Remember to use examples of the language used in the extract to show how the author gives her opinion on the topic to the reader.

PHYLLIS SCHLAFLY AND OPPOSITION TO THE WOMEN'S MOVEMENT

EXTRACT E

From a recent book on the history of the 20th century.

Some opponents wanted women to stick to the role of homemaker. As late as 1970, new organisations such as Happiness of Womanhood were being formed to support the role of woman as homemaker. Others thought that women should be putting their energy into other movements (those against poverty or racism, for example).

Reactions to the women's movement varied among both men and women. While the movement attracted some sympathisers and supporters, more frequently it encountered suspicion and insults, at least to begin with. Those who took part in protests were often verbally abused, and a few were even attacked. Media coverage was often negative, laughing at the protestors and what they were protesting against. The women's movement rarely found support from other protest movements fighting against prejudice and discrimination, as these movements shared society's traditional views of women and treated them in the same way.

Some men and women objected to any moves for greater sexual equality at all. These people believed strongly in traditional gender roles; they felt that the biological differences between women and men meant that women were naturally housewives and men their 'protectors'. They believed the women's movement and all that it stood for was very damaging to society and family life. People who were totally opposed to the women's movement often rejected all feminists as lesbians who wanted to be men or women who were too ugly to get a man!

SOURCE Q

Quotes attributed to Phyllis Schlafly.

Feminism is doomed to failure because it is based on an attempt to repeal and restructure human nature.

Sex education classes are like in-home sales parties for abortions.

Sexual harassment on the job is not a problem for virtuous women.

What I am defending is the real rights of women. A woman should have the right to be in the home as a wife and mother.

And the first commandment of feminism is: I am woman; thou shalt not tolerate strange gods who assert that women have capabilities or choose roles that are different from men's.

Far more people were opposed to some of the aims and demands of the women's movement rather than the whole movement itself. The most controversial issue was abortion and the growing calls for wider access to abortion produced an anti-feminist backlash. This drove many women to form and join protest groups in the 1970s that supported traditional roles of women as homemakers.

Anti-feminism soon had a dynamic leader in Phyllis Schlafly. Schlafly, a married mother of six, had been politically active since the 1950s, even standing for Congress in 1952. She believed that the traditional role of housewife and mother was what nature intended for women and, as a Catholic, she was a fierce opponent of abortion. Her speeches and writings managed to convince many women to join the anti-feminist cause.

"And now, our guest speaker—Phyllis Schlafly, Harvard grad, TV star and radio commentator, whose distinguished career has taken her all over the country during the past three years fighting for the need for women to stay put in the home where they belong!"

SOURCE R

A cartoon by Paul Szep which was published in the Boston Globe in 1975.

THE EQUAL RIGHTS AMENDMENT

The Equal Rights Amendment (ERA) would mean that women would be treated as totally equal and identical to men under the US Constitution. It had been presented to Congress repeatedly since 1923, but was finally passed in 1972. Schlafly founded a new organisation, 'Stop ERA', to prevent the ERA being ratified by the states. She campaigned tirelessly all over the country, highlighting her objections, such as the prospect that women would have to serve in the military and that they might lose the right to financial support from their husbands or ex-husbands. Above all, Schlafly felt the ERA would weaken the importance of the family. Her campaign delayed ratification of the ERA until the time limit was reached in 1982, when only 35 of the 38 states needed to ratify it had done so. In 2016, the ERA has still not become US law.

THE IMPACT OF THE WOMEN'S MOVEMENT

The huge range of opinion within the women's movement meant that not everything it wanted would be achieved. More moderate feminists argued that Women's Lib damaged the movement by taking away the focus from discrimination at work and equal pay. However, Women's Lib groups did help many women directly as well as helping to bring about changes, such as the legalisation of abortion. There were some other important changes. The 1972 Educational Amendment Act made all sexual discrimination in education illegal (impacting on what, as well as who, could be taught). The 1974 Equal Credit Opportunity Act made it illegal to refuse credit on the basis of gender, meaning more women could borrow money to buy things like a house, pay for education or start a business.

By 1974, more women went out to work and in a wider range of jobs than before. However, this may have been because most households needed two incomes, rather than a result of the feminist movement. The number of women in management roles remained very low and equal pay was still a dream for many. Nevertheless, the women's movement undoubtedly had an impact on the way women and men felt about gender roles. It also caused more women than ever before to become politically engaged – either in support of or opposed to the movement. Gradually it became more acceptable for a woman to have a career as well as, or even instead of, a family.

SOURCE S

The percentage of women working in various occupations, 1950–80.

▼ OCCUPATIONAL GROUP	▼ 1950	▼ 1960	▼ 1970	▼ 1980
All workers	28	33	38	44
White-collar	40	43	48	55
Professional	40	38	40	46
Managerial	14	14	17	28
Clerical	62	68	74	81
Sales	34	37	39	49
Blue-collar	24	26	30	34
Crafts	3	3	5	6
Operatives	27	28	32	34
Labourers	4	4	8	11
Private household	95	96	96	97
Other services	45	52	55	61
Farm workers	9	10	10	17

EXAM-STYLE QUESTION

A01 **A02**

SKILLS PROBLEM SOLVING, REASONING, DECISION MAKING, ADAPTIVE LEARNING, INNOVATION

'The extremism of the Women's Liberation Movement was the main reason why the women's movement failed to bring full equality for women.'

How far do you agree? Explain your answer.

You may use the following in your answer:
- the Women's Liberation Movement
- Phyllis Schlafly and opposition to the women's movement.

You **must** also use information of your own. **(16 marks)**

HINT

A good way to approach this question would be to discuss whether Women's Lib harmed the cause of greater equality for women. Then go on to discuss other reasons why greater equality was not achieved, before coming to a decision on whether Women's Lib was the main reason.

RECAP

RECALL QUIZ

1 Give three aims of student protests except for an end to the Vietnam War.
2 What was SDS?
3 What was the Berkeley Free Speech Movement campaigning for?
4 Name two leaders of the Berkeley Free Speech Movement.
5 Give three reasons why many young people protested against the Vietnam War.
6 What methods did the anti-Vietnam War movement use to protest?
7 Who were the hippies?
8 What was the name of Betty Friedan's book, which many historians believe began the women's movement?
9 What does 'feminist' mean?
10 Who was Phyllis Schlafly?

CHECKPOINT

STRENGTHEN

S1 Explain why protest movements grew in the 1960s.
S2 What was the impact of anti-Vietnam War protests on American society?
S3 What were the main aims of the women's movement and how far were these aims achieved by 1974?

CHALLENGE

C1 What was achieved by student protests?
C2 Explain why the women's movement did not achieve more of its aims.
C3 Which out of student protests, anti-Vietnam War protests and women's protests were more effective and why?

SUMMARY

- A variety of protest movements grew in the 1960s.
- Students campaigned on a wide range of issues in the 1960s and 1970s. At the heart of student protests was a rejection of the society created by their parents.
- Student protests succeeded and gave them more say in college policies and rules. They were less successful with other aims.
- The anti-Vietnam War movement united the student movement and generated some support, though it is difficult to assess whether they managed to shorten the war.
- Hippies dropped out of society altogether and created a counter-culture of peace and free-love.
- Eleanor Roosevelt tried to improve rights and opportunities for women when she was First Lady and after.
- Betty Friedan and her book *The Feminine Mystique* are credited with starting the women's movement.
- NOW used a variety of protests, such as marches, rallies, strikes and taking legal action, to enforce the Civil Rights Act and Equal Pay Act.
- The Women's Liberation Movement was more radical than NOW and wanted more fundamental changes to society.
- Many feminists campaigned for abortion to be legalised throughout the USA and, with the decision of *Roe versus Wade* in 1973, they got their wish.
- Abortion was the issue that divided the women's movement more than any other and brought much opposition.
- Opposition to the women's movement was led by Phyllis Schlafly, whose demonstrations prevented the Equal Rights Amendment from becoming law.

EXAM GUIDANCE: PART (C) QUESTIONS

A01 **A02**

SKILLS PROBLEM SOLVING, REASONING, DECISION MAKING, ADAPTIVE LEARNING, INNOVATION

Question to be answered: 'The main reason for the growth of the women's movement was the influence of the civil rights movement.'

How far do you agree? Explain your answer.

You may use the following in your answer:
- the influence of the civil rights movement
- Betty Friedan.

You **must** also use information of your own.   (16 marks)

1 Analysis Question 1: What is the question type testing?
In this question you have to demonstrate that you have knowledge and understanding of the key features and characteristics of the period studied. In this particular case, you need to show knowledge and understanding of how the women's movement in the USA grew.

You also have to explain, analyse and make judgements about historical events and periods to give an explanation and reach a judgement on the role of various factors in causing something to happen. In this particular case, you must consider why the women's movement grew.

2 Analysis Question 2: What do I have to do to answer the question well?
You have been given two topics to write about: the influence of the civil rights movement and Betty Friedan. You don't have to use the stimulus material provided, but you will find it hard to assess the role of the civil rights movement if you don't write about it! You must avoid just giving the information. You also have to say why the reasons you choose helped the women's movement to grow.

This is a 16-mark question and you need to say as much as you can in a limited time. So don't waste time with an over-lengthy introduction. A short introduction answering the question straight away and showing what your paragraphs will be is ideal. Try to use the words of the question at the beginning of each paragraph and make sure you are explaining how what you are writing about helped the women's movement to grow.

In summary to score high marks on this question you need to do three things: provide coverage of content range (at least three factors); provide coverage of arguments for and against the statement; provide clear reasons (criteria) for an overall judgement, backed by convincing argument.

Answer
Here is a student response to the question. The teacher has made some comments.

Good introduction. ───────────────→ The civil rights movement was just one of a number of reasons for the growth of the women's movement. There were other reasons that were just as important in leading to the growth of the women's movement, such as Betty Friedan's book 'The Feminine Mystique', an increasing number of well-educated women who wanted to be more than only housewives, as well as improved access and availability of birth control, which allowed women to plan their families, educations and careers.

Nice paragraph. Answers the ──────→ The civil rights movement inspired many other groups, including women, to protest to try and end discrimination and bring about a more equal society. The work of the civil rights movement had highlighted some of the inequalities in society, which led to women looking at their own lives and the discrimination they faced. Civil rights protests had received much media coverage and achieved some notable successes by the mid-1960s, which inspired women to try and achieve more equality for themselves using some similar methods to civil rights protests such as boycotts and marches.
question, gives contextual
knowledge and links the
civil rights movement to the
women's movement.

It's great that you clearly state that some people believe Betty Friedan was the main reason, rather than the civil rights movement. However, you need to prove it's the main reason by comparing it with others – not just explaining why it was important. You also need to add more on what her book and other work was about and how this led to the growth of the women's movement.

Another reason for the growth of the women's movement was Betty Friedan's best-selling book 'The Feminine Mystique'. Indeed, many historians believe that Friedan was the main reason for the growth of the women's movement, rather than the civil rights protests. The book was very influential in making women think about whether they were satisfied with their lives. Friedan also went on to found NOW, the National Organization for Women, which campaigned for gender equality.

This is quite disappointing. Although you have identified two other reasons for the growth of the women's movement, you haven't explained how these things led to an increasing number of women protesting or evaluated their importance compared to the civil rights protests.

There were other reasons for the growth of the women's movement. By the 1960s, more women than ever before were going to university and were very well educated. Also, the increased availability of contraception, such as the pill, meant that women could plan when they wanted to have their babies and therefore have an education and get good jobs too.

Good, concise finish. ───────→ In conclusion, the civil rights protests were a reason for the growth of the women's movement, but this was just one of a number of reasons and was not the most important. It was the work of Betty Friedan in highlighting gender inequality and women's unhappiness that really led to thousands of women becoming feminists.

What are the strengths and weaknesses of this answer?
You can see the strengths and weaknesses of this answer from what the teacher says. If there had been three paragraphs like the one on civil rights protests, this would have been a very good answer.

Work with a friend
Discuss with a friend how you would rewrite the weaker paragraphs in the answer to enable the whole answer to get very high marks.

Use the Student Book to set a part (c) question for a friend. Then look at the answer. Does it do the following things?

Answer checklist
- ☐ Identifies causes
- ☐ Provides detailed information to support the causes
- ☐ Shows how the causes led to the given outcome
- ☐ Provides factors other than those given in the question
- ☐ Addresses the 'main reason' by looking at arguments for and against and comparing them.

5. NIXON AND WATERGATE

LEARNING OBJECTIVES

- Understand reasons for and key features of the Watergate scandal
- Understand the impact on Nixon, US politics and new laws
- Understand why President Ford pardoned Nixon.

On 17 June 1972, five men were arrested after being caught breaking in to offices of the National Democratic Committee in the Watergate complex in Washington DC. However, this was no ordinary break-in. It would lead to a huge scandal that would rock the American political system and lead to the only resignation in history of a president of the United States.

Over a 2-year period, there were many investigations, including those by the FBI, journalists and a committee set up by Congress. These investigations discovered that many leading officials in the White House were involved in illegal activities. The trail even led to the president himself, who had lied and tried to cover up the truth on many occasions.

Watergate had a huge impact, not only on President Nixon, but also on US politics as a whole. Indeed, some effects of Watergate last to this day.

5.1 REASONS FOR AND KEY FEATURES OF THE WATERGATE SCANDAL

LEARNING OBJECTIVES

- Understand the reasons for the Watergate scandal
- Understand the key features of the Watergate scandal
- Understand why Gerald Ford gave the presidential pardon.

PRESIDENT NIXON

Richard Nixon's long political career began when he was elected to the House of Representatives in 1947. He became well-known during the Red Scare, when he was largely responsible for sending Alger Hiss for trial (see page 11), and he was elected to the Senate in 1950. Nixon served as Republican Vice President under Eisenhower (1952–60) and then ran for the presidency in 1960. He very narrowly lost to Kennedy, but was chosen by the Republicans to run again in 1968. This time he won and became president on 20 January 1969.

Nixon was very intelligent and hard-working, but he could be deeply suspicious, even **paranoid**. He was accused of holding resentments towards people he thought were against him, while rewarding people who showed loyalty. These characteristics played a central role in his presidency and led to his fall.

ACTIVITY

Write a list describing Richard Nixon's character, based on the text and Extract A. Which of these characteristics would have been positive for a president of the USA? Which of them would have been negative? Would any have been both positive and negative?

EXTRACT A

From memories of Richard Nixon by Maurice Stans (who had been Chairman of the CRP, also known as CREEP [see below], in 1972), written in 1987.

He was a man with a brilliant mind; a keen student in evaluating the pros and cons of a problem; decisive when he was satisfied with the facts before him; working at his job all the waking hours; probably the most hardworking President of this century.

He was extraordinarily sensitive to criticism; impatient with opposition; often bitter in defeat; and he was frantic over leaks.

THE WHITE HOUSE PLUMBERS AND CREEP

In June 1971, the *New York Times* published an article about the Vietnam War that was based on a series of secret documents called the **Pentagon** Papers. These documents contained confidential information about the war and had been leaked to the paper by Daniel Ellsberg, who worked at the Pentagon. Although the documents were not personally damaging to him, Nixon was furious that secret information could be revealed by someone in his administration. It increased his suspicion of others and made him worry about what else might be revealed.

KEY TERM

Pentagon the headquarters of the USA's Defense Department

Nixon set up a group called the 'White House Plumbers', whose job was to prevent more leaks of sensitive information. One of their first tasks was to 'bring down' Daniel Ellsberg. In September, some of the Plumbers broke into the office of Ellsberg's psychiatrist, looking for information they could use to discredit him. They didn't find anything useful, but the break-in showed that the Plumbers were prepared to do anything to serve their president.

EXTEND YOUR KNOWLEDGE

SCANDAL IN 1952

Watergate was not the first scandal Nixon had been involved in. When running for Vice President, he was accused of taking money from his campaign fund for personal use. He went on television and denied all charges in a speech that people called the 'Checkers' speech. Nixon said he had been given a dog called Checkers as a personal gift during the campaign. His children loved the dog and he intended to keep it! People liked what he said and he remained the vice-presidential candidate.

KEY TERMS

primaries (US political) the elections that decide which person will stand as a party's candidate for the presidency

bugging device a small piece of electronic equipment for listening secretly to other people's conversations

SOURCE A

Senator Edmund S. Muskie was the clear frontrunner in the 1972 Democratic presidential primary, when he made a mistake now known simply as the 'Muskie moment'. Muskie broke down and cried in front of reporters after allegations that his wife drank too much and swore in public. Muskie tried and failed to convince the voters that they weren't tears, but melted snowflakes, running down his cheeks. This moment is believed to have led to Muskie losing the presidential primaries.

EXTRACT B

From an article written for the *New York Times* in 2007 by one of the men who broke into the Watergate offices.

The common public perception is that Watergate was the principal cause of President Nixon's downfall. In fact, the seminal [real] cause was a first-rate criminal conspiracy and break-in almost 10 months earlier that led to Watergate and its subsequent cover-up.

THE COMMITTEE TO RE-ELECT THE PRESIDENT

In 1972, Nixon decided to stand for re-election. He set up the Committee to Re-elect the President (which popularly became known as CREEP) to raise funds for the campaign. John Mitchell, former Attorney General, was made Director of the Committee. What people didn't know at the time was that Nixon gave Mitchell a secret fund within CREEP's budget. It was to pay for the White House Plumbers to spy on and damage Nixon's potential opponents in the 1972 presidential election. They proved successful in this work. Several people who had been hoping to be the Democratic presidential candidate were disgraced. For example, the Plumbers persuaded a newspaper to publish damaging (and probably untrue) stories about Edmund Muskie's wife (see below). He broke down in tears, which is believed to have led to him losing the Democratic **primaries**.

Then, on 17 June 1972, five men were arrested after breaking in to offices of the National Democratic Committee in the Watergate complex in Washington DC. They were caught in the act of trying to repair **bugging devices** that, it was later discovered, had been installed during a previous break-in on 28 May.

THE ROLE OF THE WASHINGTON POST AND FBI IN UNCOVERING THE TRUTH

KEY TERM

White House the residence of the president of the USA. Most White House staff are employed directly by the president rather than being voted for

SOURCE B

The *Washington Post* treated Watergate as front page news from the beginning.

The burglary (break-in) initially received little attention from the press, but two reporters from the *Washington Post*, Bob Woodward and Carl Bernstein, were suspicious. They investigated and found connections to CREEP, but John Mitchell denied any link. Despite this, the journalists continued their investigation. With help from sources inside the FBI, they found more evidence that the break-in was linked to CREEP and then to the **White House**. Their reports were repeatedly denied by the White House, but Woodward and Bernstein refused to give up. They played a key role in bringing the 'Watergate' affair to the public's attention and keeping it there. They were also largely responsible for raising the suspicions of Democrat members of Congress. To begin with, Democrats accepted that the White House was not involved, but the investigative journalism of Woodward and Bernstein persuaded them that further investigations were necessary.

At the same time, the FBI was carrying out its own investigations. They quickly found links to CREEP and discovered that Howard Hunt and G. Gordon Liddy (both White House Plumbers) had played a role in planning the break-in. Gradually, over the following 2 years, the FBI revealed the extent of the campaign to spy on and sabotage Democrats. They also discovered that this campaign had been financed by CREEP. It had received donations from companies and individuals who believed they were donating to help Nixon's re-election through legal means. They had no idea their donations were being used to stage break-ins!

THE 'WATERGATE SCANDAL'

To begin with, most people considered the Watergate break-in to be a bizarre incident. Even when the five men who broke in, and Hunt and Liddy, were proved to be connected to CREEP, most people believed they were acting alone. When Nixon publicly stated that White House lawyer, John Dean, had investigated and found no one from the White House staff had been involved, most people believed him. No one thought that government officials would have anything to do with this illegal activity. Even though the Vietnam War was not going well, Nixon was widely seen as an effective president. It was no surprise when he easily won the 1972 presidential election.

On 8 January 1973, the trial of the five burglars, and Hunt and Liddy, began. They were charged with conspiracy, burglary and wiretapping. Five pleaded guilty and the other two were found guilty. All seven were due to be sentenced on 23 March. Then, amazingly, on 19 March, the trial judge received a letter from James McCord, one of the burglars and Director of Security for CREEP (Source C). It was the contents of this letter that really started the scandal, as McCord claimed that leading White House officials had told the burglars to lie during their trial.

▼ **Figure 5.1** The main people involved in the Watergate Scandal

The burglars

James McCord, Campaign Security Coordinator of CRP, former FBI and CIA agent

Bernard Barker, Estate Agent, former CIA agent, who had worked in Cuba

Frank Sturgis, worked for Barker's estate agency, former CIA agent, who had worked in Cuba

Eugenio Martinez, worked for Barker's estate agency, former CIA agent and Cuban exile

Virgilio Gonzales, Locksmith, Cuban exile

Those who planned and directed the burglary

E. Howard Hunt, a White House Plumber and member of CRP, former CIA agent

G. Gordon Liddy, a White House Plumber and member of CRP, former FBI agent

Those involved in the cover-up

Richard Nixon, President of the USA

John Mitchell, former Attorney General, then Director of CRP

John Ehrlichman, White House Assistant for Domestic Affairs and Head of the White House Plumbers

Bob Haldeman, White House Chief of Staff

John Dean, White House Lawyer

SOURCE C

An extract from the letter written by James McCord to Judge Sirica, 19 March 1973.

… in the interests of justice, and in the interests of restoring faith in the criminal justice system, which faith has been severely damaged in this case, I will state the following to you at this time which I hope may be of help to you in meting out [providing] justice in this case:

1. There was political pressure applied to the defendants to plead guilty and remain silent.
2. Perjury [lying under oath] occurred during the trial in matters relating to the… government's case, and to the motivation and intent of the defendants.
3. Others involved in the Watergate operation were not identified during the trial, when they could have been…

An extract from the *Washington Post* on 3 June 1973.

One of the strongest charges against Mr. Nixon that Dean has made to investigators refers to a meeting Dean said he had with Mr. Nixon shortly before the sentencing of the seven Watergate defendants March 23, Dean said that Mr. Nixon asked him how much the defendants would have to be paid to insure their continued silence, in addition to $460,000 that had already been paid, the sources said. Dean, the sources reported, maintains that he told Mr. Nixon the additional cost would be about $1 million, and Dean also claims the President replied there would be no problem in paying that amount.

Nixon denied that he had known that the Watergate offices were going to be burgled. On 17 April, he announced a new investigation, led by special prosecutor for the White House Archibald Cox. Then, on 30 April, Nixon announced that he had sacked Dean and Bob Haldeman (White House Chief of Staff), and that John Ehrlichman (Head of the Plumbers) had resigned, due to their part in the burglary and cover-up. Meanwhile, the Democrats had persuaded the Senate to run its own investigation. On 7 February, the Select Committee on Presidential Campaign Activities was set up. This was led by Sam Ervin, a Democratic Senator and former constitutional lawyer. In May, the investigation began, with the meetings televised across the USA. The nation was gripped and extremely shocked as people revealed the extent of the corruption at the highest level. The most shocking viewing was the 5 days of John Dean's testimony. He was the first to deliver the huge shock that the president was involved in the cover-up. Nixon refused to be questioned.

THE WATERGATE RECORDINGS

The scandal increased after one of the witnesses revealed to the committee that all conversations and phone calls in President Nixon's office had been recorded since 1971 (as all presidents since Roosevelt had done). A battle began as Archibald Cox and the Select Committee tried to get access to these recordings. Nixon constantly refused on the grounds of national security, because the recordings were about more than just Watergate. He feared it would prevent people speaking openly to the president in private again. In October 1973, he released edited scripts of some of them. The following April, he released more scripts, this time unedited except for where bad language was used (which was replaced with the words 'expletive deleted'). The public were shocked by the extent of the swearing and what was discussed.

ACTIVITY

Are you surprised by what Source D says? Explain your answer.

SOURCE E

A hearing of the Senate Select Committee on Watergate.

ACTIVITY

There were several different groups and individuals who helped to expose the Watergate scandal. For each of the following, write a paragraph explaining their role:
- FBI
- *Washington Post* reporters
- Select Committee on Presidential Campaign Activities
- James McCord
- John Dean.

The fact that Nixon would not allow access to the recordings themselves, and the discovery that some of the scripts had been cut, led the Senate to consider impeaching Nixon. Finally, on 24 July, the Supreme Court ordered Nixon to supply all the recordings. When they were played, there was sufficient evidence on them to show that Nixon had blocked the initial investigation of the Watergate break-in, abused his power and failed to obey the laws requiring him to allow access to evidence. Then, on 5 August, the 'smoking gun' was revealed – a recording from 23 June 1972 which revealed that Nixon had tried to stop the FBI investigating the break-in at the Watergate complex. This proved that he had tried to cover up Watergate from the very beginning. On 9 August, before he could be impeached, Nixon resigned.

EXAM-STYLE QUESTION

A01   **A02**

SKILLS   PROBLEM SOLVING, REASONING, DECISION MAKING, ADAPTIVE LEARNING, INNOVATION

'The most important reason the Watergate affair developed into a scandal was the televised hearings of the Senate Watergate Committee.'

How far do you agree? Explain your answer.

You may use the following in your answer:
■ the televised hearings of the Senate Watergate Committee
■ the Watergate recordings.
You **must** also use information of your own.   **(16 marks)**

HINT

You will need to read this whole section on Watergate so you can select a variety of reasons to write about in your answer. You then need to weigh up each reason to decide whether the televised hearings were the most important one.

▼ Figure 5.2 Timeline of the Watergate Scandal

17 June 1971 5 people arrested at 2:30 a.m. for the Watergate break-in

19 June 1972 The *Washington Post* reports links between the burglars and CREEP. John Mitchell denies this

1 August 1972 The *Washington Post* reports that a cheque given to CREEP was paid to one of the Watergate burglars

30 August 1972 Nixon announces that John Dean has investigated the break-in and no White House staff were involved

15 September 1972 The five burglars, plus Hunt and Liddy, are charged with conspiracy, burglary and wiretapping

11 November 1972 Nixon wins Presidential election

8–30 January 1973 Trial for the Watergate break-in

7 February 1973 Senate creates Select Committee on Presidential Campaign Activities

19 March 1973 James McCord writes to the trial judge claiming White House staff had told the burglars to lie during the trial

23 April 1973 Nixon denies advance knowledge of break-in

30 April 1973 Nixon dismisses Dean and Haldeman, Ehrlichman resigns

17 May 1973 Senate Committee hearings begin

25 June 1973 John Dean first testifies. He says Nixon was involved in the cover-up days after the break-in happened

7 July 1973 Nixon says he won't testify or grant access to files

16 July 1973 White House taping system is revealed

23 July 1973 Senate Committee demands the White House tapes and documents are handed over

25 July 1973 Nixon refuses

9 August 1973 Senate Committee begins a law suit against Nixon for failing to hand over the tapes and documents

23 October 1973 Nixon hands over some edited transcripts of the tapes

21 November 1973 A gap of nearly 20 minutes on a transcript of a conversation between Nixon and Haldeman on 20 June 1972 is discovered

6 February 1974 House of Representatives officially allows investigations on whether to impeach Nixon

24 July 1974 Supreme Court unanimously orders Nixon to release all the tapes and documents

27–30 July 1974 Investigations decide that Nixon can be impeached

5 August 1974 Final tapes are released. 23 June 1972 tape provides the 'smoking gun'

9 August 1974 Nixon resigns, Gerald Ford becomes President

GERALD FORD AND THE PRESIDENTIAL PARDON

A few hours after Nixon resigned, Vice President Gerald Ford was sworn in as president. In his first speech as president, Ford said 'our long national nightmare is over' but, for many Americans, their view of politicians had changed forever. Ford's most urgent job was to try and re-establish some faith in government and the presidency. This was no easy task but Ford's calm personality and honesty did help people to regain some confidence in the government.

Ford is remembered for one act above all others and this act is one of the reasons why Ford lost the 1976 presidential election. A month after becoming president, Ford announced that he **pardoned** Richard Nixon for any crimes he may have committed. This meant that Nixon would not face a criminal trial. It was an extremely controversial decision, as millions of Americans wanted to see Nixon brought to justice and there were still things that remained unknown. For example, it seems unlikely, but did the President know details about the burglary before it took place?

There were those who thought that Nixon and Ford had made a deal before Nixon resigned, but Ford denied this. He repeatedly stated his belief that pardoning Nixon was the only way the USA could move on from Watergate. Although it was an unpopular act, pardoning Nixon was probably the best thing to do to try and allow the nation to recover, rather than facing months, if not years, of criminal trials.

KEY TERM

pardon (v) officially allow someone who has been found guilty of a crime to go free without being punished

SOURCE F

From a speech by President Ford, 8 September 1974.

The facts, as I see them, are that a former President of the United States… would be cruelly and excessively penalized… But it is not the ultimate fate of Richard Nixon that most concerns me, my concern is the immediate future of this great country. My conscience tells me clearly and certainly that I cannot prolong the bad dreams that continue to reopen a chapter that is closed. My conscience tells me that only I, as President, have the constitutional power to firmly shut and seal this book… Now, therefore, I, Gerald R. Ford, President of the United States, pursuant to the pardon power conferred upon me by Article II, Section 2, of the Constitution, have granted and by these presents do grant a full, free, and absolute pardon unto Richard Nixon.

SOURCE G

Protestors demonstrating in Pennsylvania, on 9 September 1974, against Gerald Ford's pardon of Richard Nixon.

5.2 THE IMPACT OF WATERGATE

LEARNING OBJECTIVES

- Understand the impact of Watergate on Richard Nixon
- Understand the impact of Watergate on US politics
- Understand the new laws that were passed due to Watergate.

THE IMPACT ON NIXON

The most immediate impact of Watergate was the ending of Richard Nixon's political career. Although he said that he resigned for the good of the country, he really had little choice as impeachment seemed certain. Due to Ford's pardon, he never faced trial, but many people believed he was guilty of planning the burglary as well as covering it up.

The White House recordings did more than reveal the extent of the cover-up. They also showed the reality of life and behaviour in the president's office in a way that had never been done before. Americans were shocked at how the president spoke and thought of others. The phrase 'Expletive deleted' was used so often on the scripts that it became part of everyday language and there were numerous examples of him verbally attacking minorities, such as Jews and Italians. Another issue was that Nixon never apologised or admitted doing anything wrong. He didn't seem to think that he had done anything worse than other presidents had before him. He even appeared to believe that presidents should not be answerable to the law.

EXTEND YOUR KNOWLEDGE

HIDING THE TRUTH

Richard Nixon's character and behaviour had been totally exposed by Watergate in a way that former presidents had never been. Indeed, some aspects of the lives of previous presidents had been kept hidden from the public at least during their time in office. Therefore, most Americans never knew the extent of Franklin Roosevelt's disability – he was only able to walk a few steps with the help of leg braces and crutches. Nor did they know of Kennedy's unfaithfulness to his wife or Johnson's impolite behaviour. Indeed, President Johnson used to have meetings with government officials while sitting on the toilet, with the door open!

ACTIVITY

In May 1977, a few years after Watergate, there was a very famous series of television interviews with Richard Nixon by the British journalist David Frost. In these interviews Nixon was very open in his replies. If possible, watch some of these interviews on the internet. How do you think the American public would have reacted to them?

There were some important achievements of Nixon's presidency. For example, he led important environmental actions, such as setting up the Environment Protection Agency, and, unlike previous presidents, he managed to enforce the desegregation of schools. In foreign policy, his efforts led to improved relations with both China and the Soviet Union. However, after his resignation, none of these achievements seemed to matter. Everything except Watergate was ignored. His reputation was totally destroyed and people called him 'Tricky Dicky'. ('Dicky' is an abbreviation of the name Richard.) In later years, he did regain some respect. He became a well-regarded author and was frequently invited to give speeches at different events, particularly on foreign affairs, in which he was considered an expert. Future presidents also consulted him for advice. However, most people only remember Nixon for Watergate and he frequently tops polls for the worst or least popular president in American history.

EXTRACT C

From a British newspaper article on the legacy of Richard Nixon, published 4 January 2013.

Substantial as his presidential achievements were, they became completely overshadowed by the dishonour of Watergate. Although Nixon had no foreknowledge of the burglary of the Democratic National Offices by the White House "plumbers", he created the atmosphere in which it could happen. He participated in the cover-up knowingly and lied about it repeatedly. Some of his Oval Office conversations... on the White House tapes [recordings], were unbelievably... sleazy. [These combined horrors were] "a breach of faith" between the president and the American people. This is why Nixon had to go...

SOURCE H

A cartoon published in the *New York Post*, 14 May 1973.

THE IMPACT ON US POLITICS

Watergate hit American politics in many different ways, both positive and negative, for the short and the long term.

Nixon may have escaped criminal punishment, but many government officials were tried and over 30 received prison sentences (including all the people in Figure 5.1). This meant there was a massive change in government staff. The Republican Party tried to distance itself from Nixon and his advisers, but still suffered badly at the next elections, losing a large number of seats in the House of Representatives and some seats in the Senate. For the next presidential election, the Democrats chose the relatively unknown Jimmy Carter as their candidate because he was likable, honest, religious and was not seen as part of 'the Washington set'. Carter won the election even though he lacked the skills to be a strong president. Some historians have argued that Watergate has caused American voters to value honesty more than capability in their presidential candidates ever since.

Watergate caused the American people to lose trust in their government. Both Republicans and Democrats were believed to be corrupt and possibly even criminal. In the months and years after Watergate, many politicians began publishing their financial records and opening meetings to the public to show that they were honest. However, the damage had been done. Watergate led to fewer people voting and wanting to become politicians. It also became more difficult to recruit officials to work for political parties or the Federal government.

SOURCE I

The percentage of Americans who said they would trust the Federal government to do the right thing.

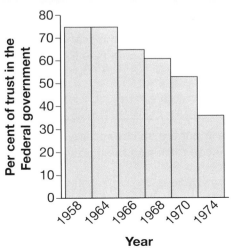

EXTRACT D

From a history of the modern world, published in 2001.

... the deeper damage of Watergate was that it undermined confidence in politics. It seemed as if political leadership had been replaced by... manipulation. Some people could not believe that these events were taking place in the USA. The question was whether Nixon was a corrupt one-off or whether this kind of behaviour was an inevitable part of the political system. People feared that the problem ran deep. Stirring up and uncovering scandal became a preoccupation of the press. The confidence and idealism of the 1960s were replaced by doubt and cynicism.

Watergate also had a significant impact on the media. The role of Bernstein and Woodward in finding out the truth was widely praised and many journalists focused on trying to uncover more scandal in the years following. This was positive, as political parties and individuals were subject to more focus than previously. However, it was also negative as journalists were often quick to publish 'scandals' without having the evidence to support them.

NEW LAWS

In an attempt to try and prevent something like Watergate happening again, and in particular to prevent future presidents from acting without the approval of Congress, a number of new laws were passed.
- 1973 House and Senate Open Meeting Rules – all committee meetings had to be open to the public.
- 1973 War Powers Act – stopped a president going to war without Congress' approval.
- 1974 Election Campaign Act – set limits on election campaign spending and contributions.
- 1974 Freedom of Information Act – gave people the right to access any government documents in which they featured.
- 1974 Privacy Act – set rules on how the government could collect information on individuals.
- 1974 Congressional Budget Control Act – set rules on how the president could use government money.

These additional laws have helped, and will continue to help, prevent another Watergate. However, it was also hoped that the changes in legislation would help restore faith in government. This is far more difficult to measure, but Watergate certainly removed the 'myth' about the morality and honesty of anyone holding the office of president. Another outcome of the scandal is that '-gate' has become a suffix for any scandal around the world (see Extend).

EXTEND YOUR KNOWLEDGE

'GATE'

Since the Watergate scandal, the suffix '-gate' has been added to hundreds of other scandals all over the world. Some of the most famous are: 'Camillagate' (1993) for the scandal that happened after the publication of a script of a phone call between the British Prince Charles and Camilla Parker Bowles; 'Monicagate' (1998) for the scandal of an affair between US President Bill Clinton and a White House intern, Monica Lewinsky.

ACTIVITY

1 Create a mind map of how Watergate impacted on US politics.
2 In pairs or small groups, discuss what you think was the greatest impact of Watergate.
3 What is the message of Source H?

RECAP

RECALL QUIZ

1 What was the CRP (also known as CREEP)?
2 How many people were first put on trial for the Watergate break-in?
3 Name the two journalists from the *Washington Post* credited with uncovering much of the truth behind the Watergate break-in.
4 How did James McCord's actions lead to the Watergate affair becoming a scandal?
5 What was the name of the Senate's investigation committee on Watergate?
6 When did Nixon resign?
7 Why did Ford pardon Nixon?
8 Name three White House officials, except Nixon, who were part of the cover-up.
9 Why were many new laws passed after Watergate?
10 What did the Election Campaign Act do?

CHECKPOINT

STRENGTHEN

S1 Explain why the Watergate affair became such a huge scandal.
S2 Explain why Nixon had to resign.
S3 Explain three impacts of the Watergate scandal.

CHALLENGE

C1 What were the most significant events in Nixon's downfall?
C2 Explain three short-term and three longer-term impacts of the Watergate scandal.
C3 What caused the greater scandal – the illegal activities ordered by government officials or the attempts to cover them up afterwards?

SUMMARY

■ President Nixon was paranoid about people leaking sensitive information to the press and set up the White House Plumbers to stop this.
■ The Committee to Re-elect the President (CRP or CREEP) was set up to raise funds for Nixon's re-election campaign in 1971.
■ The White House Plumbers were paid by CREEP to spy on and damage Nixon's potential rivals in the presidential election.
■ On 17 June 1972, five men were arrested while repairing bugging devices previously fitted in the National Democratic Committee's office in the Watergate complex. They were quickly linked to CREEP and some White House staff, but Nixon and others repeatedly denied any White House staff were involved.
■ Bob Woodward and Carl Bernstein from the *Washington Post* played a major role in keeping Watergate in the press and raising its profile so Congress decided to investigate.
■ Before his sentencing, one of the burglars, James McCord, told the judge in a letter that leading officials in the White House had told the burglars to lie in court.
■ The Select Committee on Presidential Activities began televised hearings in May 1973 and the extent of the corruption began to be revealed.
■ Nixon fiercely fought the committee, who demanded access to the recordings of all conversations in his office.
■ The Supreme Court finally ordered Nixon to hand over all the recordings.
■ Nixon resigned on 9 August 1974 and Gerald Ford became president.
■ Ford granted Nixon a presidential pardon, so he didn't face criminal trial.
■ To try and restore public faith in the government and prevent another Watergate, Congress passed new laws limiting the president's power, setting limits on campaign spending and setting rules on how information on individuals can be collected.

EXAM GUIDANCE: PART (C) QUESTIONS

A01   **A02**

SKILLS PROBLEM SOLVING, REASONING, DECISION MAKING, ADAPTIVE LEARNING, INNOVATION

Question to be answered: 'The main impact of the Watergate scandal was a lack of trust in politicians and government.'

How far do you agree? Explain your answer.

You may use the following in your answer:
- lack of trust in politicians and government
- new laws, including the Election Campaign Act (1974).

You **must** also use information of your own.   (16 marks)

1 Analysis Question 1: What is the question type testing?
In this question you have to demonstrate that you have knowledge and understanding of the key features and characteristics of the period studied. In this particular case, you need to show knowledge and understanding of the impacts of the Watergate scandal. You also have to explain, analyse and make judgements about historical events and periods to give an explanation and reach a judgement on the main consequences of something.

2 Analysis Question 2: What do I have to do to answer the question well?
You don't have to use the stimulus material provided, but you will find it hard to assess the impact of a lack of trust in politicians and government if you don't write about it! You must avoid just giving the information. You also have to say how the Watergate scandal had that effect.

This is a 16-mark question and you need to say as much as you can in a limited time. So don't waste time with an over-lengthy introduction. A short introduction answering the question straight away and showing what your paragraphs will be is ideal. Try to use the words of the question at the beginning of each paragraph and make sure you are explaining how what you are writing about shows an impact of Watergate.

In summary, to score high marks on this question you need to do three things: provide coverage of content range (at least three factors); provide coverage of arguments for and against the statement; provide clear reasons (criteria) for an overall judgement, backed by convincing argument.

 Answer
Here is a student response to the question. The teacher has made some comments.

Good concise introduction, where you clearly state your opinion.

I agree that the main impact of the Watergate scandal was a lack of trust in politicians and government. There were several other important consequences of Watergate, such as the resignation of President Nixon (the only time a president has ever resigned) and the trial and imprisonment of over 30 government officials. However, the consequential lack of trust in politicians and government had very long-lasting and damaging effects, which makes it the most important impact.

Nice paragraph. Answers the question, gives contextual knowledge explaining how Watergate caused this lack of trust and explains why it was the main impact.

Before the Watergate Scandal, most Americans trusted that their president and members of Congress were trustworthy and trying to do the right thing. The Watergate Scandal changed this enormously as it caused Americans to completely lose faith in their government. The Watergate affair showed that US officials were capable of breaking the law to get what they wanted, which shocked many people; however, what was perhaps most damaging was that the president and many other government workers repeatedly lied and tried to cover up what had happened. This had the impact of making all politicians seem to be corrupt and dishonest. It was the main impact because this distrust of politicians lasts to this day.

It's good that you've included your own information and another impact of Watergate, but you don't explain how Watergate led to Nixon's resignation.

Another impact of the Watergate scandal was that it led to the resignation of President Nixon. This was very significant as it was the first, and only, time that a president has ever resigned – but this impact did not last as long as the lack of trust in politicians did.

You give another of your own examples of the consequences of Watergate, which is good: there is no need to use both bullet points if you don't want to.

President Nixon was not the only person to lose his job because of Watergate, several other officials resigned or were sacked. Moreover, over 30 government officials were sent to prison for taking part in illegal acts such as organising the break-in, spying on people or trying to cover it up afterwards. This was important as it had never been done before and it also meant that many experienced White House staff were not there to help run the country in the years afterwards.

It's not a good idea to introduce new ideas (the new laws passed) in your conclusion that you haven't discussed during the rest of the essay.

In conclusion, the main impact of the Watergate scandal was a lack of trust in politicians and government. Although there were several important consequences of Watergate, such as the new laws passed to try and stop government corruption, the lack of trust lasted for many, many years. It stopped people voting and wanting to become politicians, which meant that it damaged the US political system.

What are the strengths and weaknesses of this answer?

You can see the strengths and weaknesses of this answer from what the teacher says. This would have been a very good answer with a few more details added to some paragraphs and an improved conclusion.

Work with a friend

Discuss with a friend how you would rewrite the weaker paragraphs in the answer to enable the whole answer to get very high marks.

Use the Student Book to set a part (c) question for a friend. Then look at the answer. Does it do the following things?

Answer checklist

☐ Explains a number of impacts
☐ Provides an impact not listed in the question
☐ Tries to reach an overall judgement.

GLOSSARY

accusation a statement saying that someone is guilty of a crime or of doing something wrong

acquittal an official statement in a court of law that someone is not guilty

activist someone who works hard doing practical things to achieve social or political change

ally/allies friend, or nations who are fighting together in an alliance

atomic bomb a bomb with enormous destructive power, due to the sudden release of energy caused by the splitting of the nuclei of the chemical plutonium or uranium

bail money left with a court of law to make sure a person will return when their trial starts

bill (political) a proposed law. A bill has to be passed by Congress and approved by the president and Supreme Court before it becomes law. When it has been passed, a bill becomes an Act

buffer zone an area between two armies, that is intended to separate them so that they do not fight

cabinet politicians with important positions in a government who meet to make decisions or advise the leader of the government

campaign (n) a series of actions (such as battles) intended to achieve a particular result

catalyst something or someone that causes an event to happen

Catholic belonging or relating to the part of the Christian religion whose leader is the Pope

civil war a conflict between two opposing sides in the same country

Cold War a conflict that never involves physical fighting between the two sides

concession something that you allow someone to have in order to end an argument or a disagreement

conspiracy a secret plan made by two or more people to do something that is harmful or illegal

contempt in this sense, not respecting the authority of HUAC

convicted proven or officially announced as guilty of a crime after a trial in a law court

corrupt dishonest or illegal

cover-up (n) an attempt to protect someone by hiding unpleasant facts about them

curfew zone an area where people are forced to stay indoors at particular times

death penalty the legal punishment of death

debate discussion of a particular subject that often continues for a long time and in which people express different opinions

defendant the person in a court of law who has been accused of doing something illegal

defense the act of protecting something or someone from attack (American spelling)

desegregation ending a system in which people of different races are kept separate

detention camp a place where people are kept for a particular reason, when they do not want to be there

discrimination treating people unfairly because of their group or class

empire a group of countries that are all controlled by one ruler or government

executed killed deliberately, especially legally as a punishment

extremist someone who has extreme political opinions and aims, and who is willing to do unusual or illegal things in order to achieve them

First Lady wife of the US president

footage cinema film

Great Depression the economic depression of the 1930s after the Wall Street stock market crashed in 1929 which sent many Americans into poverty

harassed/harassment (n) when someone behaves in an unpleasant or threatening way towards you

highway a wide main road that joins one town to another

hindsight the ability to understand a situation only after it has happened

Hispanic from or relating to countries where Spanish or Portuguese are spoken, especially ones in Latin America

Hollywood a part of Los Angeles in California where films are made, often used to refer to the film industry in general

hypocritical behaving in a way that is different from what you claim to believe – used to show disapproval

hysteria a situation in which a lot of people feel fear, anger, or excitement, which makes them behave in an unreasonable way

imperial power the rule of an emperor or empress over an empire

innocence (legal) the fact of being not guilty of a crime

intervene to become involved in a difficult situation in order to change what happens

jail not bail a tactic of not paying bail to be released from police custody and being sent to prison instead. This was done because paying bail would be seen as accepting they had done something wrong. It also filled the jails to gain maximum attention

Jim Crow name used for the system of racial segregation in the USA 1877–1960s

jury a group of ordinary people who listen to the details of a case in court and decide whether someone is guilty or not

leak deliberately give secret information to a newspaper, television company, etc.

legal proceedings the use of the legal system (laws) to settle an argument, put right an unfair situation etc

legislature law-making body

liberation movement a body of people fighting for freedom from conditions that make their lives difficult, unfair or unhappy

moderate having opinions or beliefs, especially about politics, that are not extreme and that most people consider reasonable

Native American someone who belongs to one of the races that lived in North America before Europeans arrived

Nazis the National Socialist Party of Adolf Hitler, which controlled Germany from 1933 to 1945

negotiator someone who takes part in official discussions, especially in business or politics, in order to try and reach an agreement

nomination the act of officially suggesting someone or something for a position, duty, or prize, or the fact of being suggested for it

nuclear disarmament the process or activity of getting rid of nuclear weapons

opinion poll the process of asking a large group of people the same questions in order to find out what most people think about something

overrule to change an order or decision that you think is wrong, using your official power

paranoid obsessively anxious, suspicious and full of distrust

petition a written request signed by a lot of people, asking someone in authority to do something or change something

police escort when a group of police officers or vehicles go with someone in order to protect or guard them

poll tax a tax of a particular amount that is collected from every citizen of a country

pressure group a group or organisation that tries to influence the opinions of ordinary people and persuade the government to do something

privilege a special advantage that is given only to one person or group of people

prosecution the process or act of bringing a charge against someone for a crime, or of being judged for a crime in a court of law

Protestant a member of a part of the Christian Church that separated from the Roman Catholic Church in the 16th century

racism prejudice and discrimination against someone because of their race

rallies large public meetings, especially ones held outdoors to support a political idea, protest etc

reform changes made in order to improve things

resign (political) officially announce that you have decided to leave your job or an organisation

resistance fighting against someone who is attacking you or against new ideas or changes

riot a situation in which a large crowd of people are behaving in a violent and uncontrolled way, especially when they are protesting about something

satellite state a country which is officially independent but under the heavy influence or control of another country

segregation separating or keeping people apart, in this case along racial lines

slogan a short phrase that is easy to remember and is used in advertisements, or by politicians, organisations etc

Soviet Union officially known as the Union of Soviet Socialist Republics, the Soviet Union was a federation containing many states, the largest being Russia, which existed between 1922 and 1991

State Department the US Federal government department responsible for foreign policy, led by the Secretary of State

subversion working to harm or destroy something, in this case, US society

superpower a nation that has very great military and political power

sympathiser someone who supports the aims of an organisation or political party

taxation the system of charging taxes

traitor someone who acts against the best interests of their own country

Treasury the government department in charge of the money that a country collects in taxes and from borrowing, and the money that it spends

troops soldiers in an organised group

United Nations an international organisation, which was set up in 1945 so countries could work together to solve problems and conflicts

uprising an attempt by a group of people to change the government or laws

versus used to show that two people or teams are competing against each other in a game or court case

veto to reject or refuse the decisions of another

INDEX